Home Video

Richard Dean

Newnes Technical Books

Newnes Technical Books
is an imprint of the Butterworth Group
which has principal offices in
London, Boston, Durban, Singapore, Sydney, Toronto, Wellington

First published 1982

© Butterworth & Co. (Publishers) Ltd, 1982

British Library Cataloguing in Publication Data

Dean, Richard
  Home video.
  1. Video tape recorders and recording
  I. Title
  621.389'32   TK6655.V5

  ISBN 0-408-01166-1

Photoset by Butterworths Litho Preparation Department
Printed in England by Page Bros. Ltd., Norwich, Norfolk

Contents

1

What is video recording?

The technique of video recording was, until quite recently, confined to professional users. Companies with a sales or training message to circulate have found video to be a compact and convenient method of doing so. For some years, much of what appears on television has been recorded on videotape. Now video – literally meaning 'I see' – has become a household word with the advent of inexpensive home video recorders. As a medium, however, it is still widely misunderstood. Many people consider video as technically complicated and fear that elaborate care is involved, or are simply wondering what it is.

Video recording is the storage of electronic pictures and sound on magnetic tape. In practical terms, it offers more than this rather dry description. It can mean more control over your social life, the chance to build up a 'library' of television and a new way of capturing unique moments in your life with a video camera.

One of the best ways to describe video is to make a comparison with film. Whereas film must be processed to view, videotape can be played back immediately after it has been recorded. Unwanted recordings can be simply recorded over, in the same way as audio cassettes. The finished tape is viewed on an ordinary television set, without the need for a projector or special screen. The video recorder both records and plays back the tape. You can load or remove videotape cassettes without winding back to the beginning; though for storage it is always best to do so to maintain an even tension on the tape. Sound is automatically recorded alongside the picture tracks on a videotape, as with Super 8 home movie film systems.

1

Video's immediate attraction, however, is its ability to record TV broadcasts and switch on and off under timer control. This means you can set a machine to record programmes in your absence leaving you free to do other things.

The basic home recorder

Video recorders vary in the type of recording format used. VHS (Video Home System), Betamax, and Video 2000 are the most modern, but there are others which are described later. All machines plug straight into the mains. Once the clock has been set to the correct time, the machine is left permanently plugged in. If you are concerned about the fire risk, consider that the clock uses less power than a kitchen wall clock. In normal 'standby' mode, only the clock is activated. If power is interrupted, the clock and timer settings are lost in all but the most recent models. When power is returned, the machine warns you of this by flashing the clock display rapidly.

Connection to the TV set is by means of a single cable supplied with the recorder. This plugs in to the aerial socket of the TV and the output coaxial socket on the recorder. The aerial is plugged in to a labelled input socket on the machine.

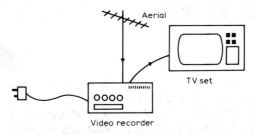

Connecting a video recorder to the TV. The aerial plugs straight into the machine. A coaxial lead links the recorder to the TV

The aerial signal is not affected by passing through the recorder and you can view programmes normally whether the machine is in use or not. Contrary to popular belief, you do not need a special adaptor to replay video recordings. The only point to make is that it is preferable to use a TV set equipped with a 'video' or 'VR' channel to view recorded programmes.

2

This channel is more tolerant to the instability most recorders exhibit in relation to directly broadcast programmes. Many televisions are tolerant on all channels; it is best to check this out with your dealer.

The recorder takes its signal straight from the aerial; it does not 'record from the television' as some people believe. Consequently, it is unnecessary to switch the television on while a recording is being made. The recorder is completely independent.

Operating controls

The main controls are best likened to an audio cassette deck. Play, wind, rewind, stop and record are self explanatory, but you will also find 'audio dub' on most machines. This allows you to record or 'dub' a new soundtrack on to an existing video recording without affecting the picture and is invaluable for home video movie-making.

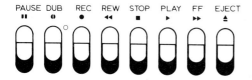

The operating controls of a JVC 3320 VHS recorder

On audio cassette machines the recording heads, guides and pinch wheel move towards the tape to play or record the cassette. On a video recorder, it is the tape that moves. A loading mechanism pulls tape out of the cassette and wraps it around a spinning drum containing the heads on the most popular ('helical scan') machines. Some machines also keep the tape 'laced-up' in this way during wind and rewind. To remove the cassette you must press an additional button marked 'cassette' or 'eject'.

The remaining controls mainly concern the timer section. Their complexity varies enormously according to the facilities on the machine, but all allow the times of a start and stop recording period to be set in advance. Some timers accept instructions for up to eight periods with channel changing if

3

necessary, up to two weeks in advance. A timer's ease of operation is important – you may find some easy, and others difficult. This question is discussed in detail later.

All video recorders have a tuning section with channel selector buttons, in exactly the same way as a television. These are adjusted to receive broadcast television stations in a simple sequence described later. Some video recorders have electronic station seeking built into the tuner, obviating the need for tuning pre-sets and, usually, channel buttons.

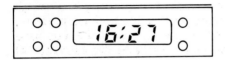

A simple video recorder timer unit

You will see that the main controls of a video recorder fall into three categories: tape transport, timer and tuner. To a lesser or greater extent, manufacturers follow the same logic in the design of these controls. They differ radically in style – from mechanical to touch-sensitive to remote control – and may take a little time to get used to. Essentially, however, operating a video recorder is not difficult.

Using the recorder

Video recorder use falls into three categories: 'timeshifting', television library building, videogram playing, and home video movies. Probably the most popular is timeshifting, when the machine is used to record programmes which clash with another channel, or are on at an inconvenient time, to play back at your leisure. A problem can be to find the time to watch all your recordings, as your dependency on the television set decreases.

A general point most people make is that they have watched less television since using a video recorder. You become more selective. Rather than spend a whole evening 'in front of the box', the tendency is to pick out interesting programmes for recording. The video recorder really can be a very liberating device. Television library building similarly requires intelligent use of the timer. A range of tapes can be assembled, contain-

4

ing anything from all of Hitchcock's broadcast films to a whole series on gardening hints. Videograms offer a direct alternative to broadcast television, while home video movies are ultimately the most fulfilling use to which video can be put.

Timeshifting television broadcasts

Timeshifting is very economical on tape. At a pinch, you might only need one 3 or 4 hour tape and the longest tapes are the cheapest per hour. You can record an evening's viewing, taking in a film, a documentary programme and a chat show, for instance, on one tape. The beauty of it is that after you have watched those programmes, you can rewind the tape and set the machine for another timeshift. The problem is to find the time to watch the tapes. It is not uncommon to record programmes and never watch them.

Another difficulty is when a programme you want to keep emerges among a batch of mediocre items. It is sometimes difficult to tailor other good programmes around it and so make the most of the tape. Having been recording television broadcasts for some years now, I have found that the most efficient way to use both tape and machine is to make all the recordings on the assumption that they are permanent; the television library approach.

Taping a television library

Films rarely last for more than 1½ hours and the library builder may prefer to buy 2 hour cassettes for this purpose. The shorter tapes are more expensive per hour but, with adequate labelling, you can generate an enviable store of programmes or notable films to enjoy with friends and family. Unfortunately the broadcasters' scheduling punctuality often leaves a lot to be desired. So for really important items, it may be worth supervising the recording. Films broadcast on the independent networks are frequently cut whereas BBC films as a rule are not; another problem with independent television material is of course the commercial breaks.

If you decide to use the timer, always set the switch-off time for five minutes after the published end of the programme. This takes care of most routine punctuality errors. Programmes

5

are rarely broadcast ahead of schedule, though it is extremely annoying when that does happen. I have been campaigning for years that broadcasters emit an electronic cue on an unused part of the TV picture to trigger video recorders. They are loath to do so – not least because of the legal uncertainty surrounding television recording – although manufacturers would co-operate.

Tapes can be recorded from the TV . . .

When using the channel-switching timers found on more expensive machines, be sure the programmes you set do not clash. This may sound obvious but some timers do not warn you of incorrect setting and simply make a random choice of which recording to make. Every video cassette has a removable tab or switch to prevent accidental erasure of treasured recordings.

Playing videograms

The range of pre-recorded tapes or videograms is expanding all the time. Although the period between cinema and television screening is being reduced, a number of films have been released on tape while still current in the cinema. Categories cover anything from feature films and pop music to sport instruction. Videograms can offer a genuine change from the same old TV schedules. The existence of pornography underlines among other things the concept of videograms as a television alternative.

There are three ways of watching videograms. You can buy, rent, or join a club. The club method involves paying a subscription entitling you to a number of tapes each year in sequence. It is cheaper than renting, but titles are subject to availability. You cannot be certain of receiving a specific tape on request. Membership typically costs around £75 for 24 tapes a year. To rent a feature film tape costs £6 or so for 3 days hire, while to buy would cost about £40. However specialised tapes – from sports action to pop performances – can be bought for between £20 and £30.

. . . and hired or bought from dealers to build your own library

Unfortunately videogram quality can vary enormously. You are advised to deal with reputable distributors offering some form of guarantee. Two stages are critical in the production of tapes. A master tape is made initially from original video 'takes', or copied from a 35 mm original in the case of a feature film. Videograms originated on video are usually of good quality at the master tape stage. Film copies are more variable. The original film should be cleaned and colour corrected for frame consistency. It is then transferred to a video master tape on sophisticated telecine equipment of the sort used by broadcasters to show films on television. The master tape is then transferred on to production masters and commercial copies made on a bank of modified home video machines. Here the sound quality must be optimised or you may experience a muddy, distorted effect.

Tracking accuracy of the video heads relative to the tape must be correctly adjusted also, or the picture will be unstable. Most video recorders have a 'tracking' control designed to cope with discrepancies in the video track angle of tapes not recorded on that machine. In badly copied tapes, the tracking control cannot make enough adjustment to the angle of tracking, and picture break-up results.

Another flaw to watch for is dropout. This appears as fine horizontal white lines darting across the screen. All video recorders have dropout compensators to replace missing lines, but their capacity is limited. Too much dropout on a tape results in some dropout being seen on the screen. All these defects are typical of the 'cowboy' videogram retailer who often uses pirated material. They should be avoided at all costs.

Making home movies on video

Home video is not just a passive experience. Unlike almost any other leisure innovation, it offers both entertainment and opportunity for participation. A video system is capable of capturing some of the most precious moments in life. Some thought should be given to this aspect when buying equipment, even by those normally disinterested in home movie-making. The reason is based on cost. Whereas the Super-8 cine enthusiast needs a complete kit of specialised equipment, the video user has much already at hand. The household television is your screen, and the video recorder your projector. If you buy a portable recorder with separate tuner timer initially, this gives you the nucleus of a television recording and movie-making set-up. This combination may be a little more expensive than an ordinary mains video recorder, but prepares you for movie-making. All you need to complete the basic system is a colour camera, of which there are many on the market.

Another reason for giving movie-making in video some consideration is how quickly you can learn from it. Video is an instant medium and mistakes made are seen on tape seconds later. So you learn quicker than if you had to wait for film to be

8

processed. It is often possible to re-shoot a clumsily taken scene 'in the field' and return home with a tape you know to be at least passable. Note that videotape can be erased again and again and tape costs are far lower than film. Home movie-making is a fascinating aspect of video which is discussed in considerable detail later in the book.

2

Video formats

From the very beginning of video's evolution, there has always been a conflict of formats. What is a 'format' exactly? It is simply a particular set of variables (or specifications if you like) relating to a certain method of doing something, in this case storing television pictures and sound. Why have formats become such an issue in video? Why not agree on one standard so that questions of format can be forgotten and all tapes and machines will be compatible with each other?

The reasons why this has not happened are various; but they essentially boil down to two factors. One is the *laissez-faire* spirit that often accompanies a pioneered technology, fuelled by the gains to be made by the format 'winner'. The other is that the technology itself depends heavily on other developments – notably in the field of micro-electronics – which have themselves made great strides during video's short life.

Following the fundamental discovery of electromagnetism (see *How video works*), experiments to record television pictures began with equipment using vast amounts of tape passing a stationary recording head at high speed. The BBC experimented with a system called VERA (Vision Electronic Recording Apparatus) using this principle in 1952. In 1956, however, largely due to the efforts of Ray Dolby (whose name is perhaps better known to hi-fi enthusiasts for his work on noise reduction), Ampex Corporation of America unveiled a system called 'Quadhead transverse recording'. This involved a radical new technique. Instead of propelling tape at a cumbersomely high speed past a fixed head, Ampex struck on the idea of moving the heads as well as the tape to achieve the high tape-to-head speed required. Four video heads mounted in

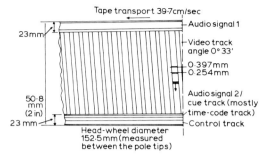

The Quadruplex recording format

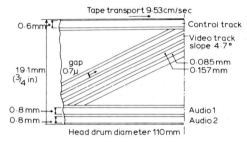

The U-matic recording format

opposite pairs on a rotating drum were spun at right angles across a 2in tape. Sound was recorded conventionally along the edge of the tape. The system was refined and, as Quadruplex, has become a standard format of the broadcasting industry.

These recorders cost thousands of pounds, however, and it was not until the development of 'helical scan' recording that the prospect of video could be contemplated anywhere outside the professional television studio. Instead of recording at a right angle, helical scan machines record video signals diagonally across the tape. The name 'helical' comes from the position of the video tracks *in situ* with the head drum, around which the tape is wrapped. Only two heads are needed, each taking over from the other in turn, so the width of the tape could be reduced. A variety of reel-to-reel helical formats flourished until Sony introduced a cassette system called U-matic in 1971. This was aimed at the home user but size and price were prohibitive. The format has since become very established in industry and commerce for training and programme storage.

11

VCR and VCR-LP

In 1972 Philips Industries of Holland introduced the first home video recorder: the VCR format N1500 series machine. This used ½in tape on coaxial spools (one above the other) and contained a crude timer for absentee recording on which you could set a switch-on time up to 24 hours ahead. The tape cassette could only record up to 1 hour of television, however,

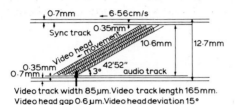

Video track width 85μm. Video track length 165mm.
Video head gap 0·6 μm. Video head deviation 15°

N1700 recording system

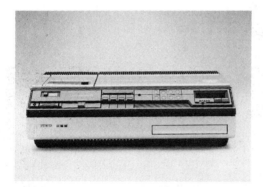

The Philips N1700 recording format and the
machine

which made the format both expensive and of limited use to the home user. Using a lapsed Japanese patent, Philips incorporated a technique called 'slant-azimuth recording' to produce a long play version of VCR format in 1977. The VCR-LP format (N1700 series machines) could record up to 2½h (later 3h with thinner tape) on a standard VCR cassette by dispensing with guard bands between adjacent video tracks. By tilting each video head in opposite directions (±15° on VCR-LP) away from true azimuth (where the head gap is at a perfect right angle to its plane of motion), the interference or 'crosstalk'

12

caused by a head erring into an adjacent track belonging to the other head was minimised. If you own an audio cassette deck you will find that by tilting the playback head (there is usually screw adjustment) the sound definition, that is the top frequency response, will be significantly reduced. That principle is exploited in the slant-azimuth technique, now used on all home video recording formats. Phasing circuits remove lower frequency crosstalk. The otherwise essential guard bands were replaced with more video information in this way to yield an extended playing time. VCR-LP and VCR recordings are hence mutually incompatible.

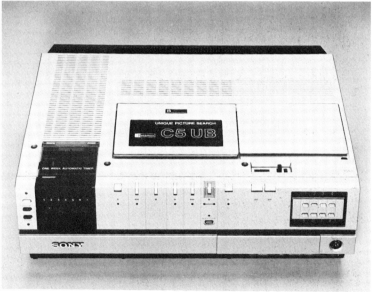

Betamax lacing and the Sony C5 UB machine

Betamax

Meanwhile the Japanese were busily working on what was initially a united answer to the Dutch home video formats. A system using ½in tape on coplanar (side by side) spools was under development by Sony in co-operation with the giant Matsushita Electric Corporation (known here as Panasonic). To Sony's astonishment, Matsushita rejected its system at a late stage. Sony decided to go ahead on its own with what was to become known as the Betamax system in mid 1978. Later that year, Matsushita's ambivalence to Sony's Betamax became clear. The Victor Corporation of Japan (JVC) – in which Matsushita has a controlling interest – launched its own VHS (Video Home System) cassette format.

VHS

VHS was remarkably similar to Betamax, using ½in tape on coplanar spools in a casing not much bigger than the Betamax

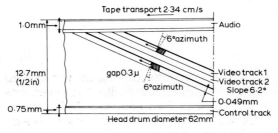

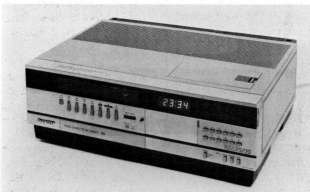

The VHS recording format and the Sharp VC7300H recorder

14

cassette. VHS was to gain more manufacturer and brand loyalty than Betamax or indeed any other home video system to date. Apart from minor changes in tape speed, video head speed and video track width, VHS and Betamax had little technically between them – except in one important respect. During fast forward and reverse winding, Betamax tape remains laced around the head drum. On a VHS machine, tape is returned to the cassette in these modes. While some argued that head and tape wear was consequently greater on a Betamax machine, the difference nevertheless allowed the Betamax manufacturer, Toshiba, to introduce the first recorder with 'cue and review' – jargon for a fast-winding-with-picture facility – in 1980. Shortly afterwards Sony incorporated this feature in its deluxe C7 recorder, together with another first, a programmable timer. This timer is capable of accepting several recording instructions and changing channels automatically. VHS soon caught up, however, as Panasonic introduced its NV-7000 with Dolby noise-reduced soundtrack, plus cue and review, and longer maximum playing time of 4 h instead of Betamax's 3¼ h.

SVR

Grundig, the German consumer electronics giant part-owned by Philips, entered the home video scene with deluxe versions of Philips' VCR format recorder. Two years after Philips introduced the VCR-LP, Grundig decided to launch its own variation using chrome-formulation VCR tapes supplied exclusively by Germany's BASF. The format was to be called SVR (Super Video Recorder) and offered 4 hr recording time as against Philips 3 hr maximum on VCR-LP.

SVR cassettes are dimensionally identical to the VCR series cassettes and can be used on VCR or VCR-LP machines. Standard VCR series tapes however cannot be used on the SVR system because they lack the short plastic bridge used to denote SVR chrome tapes. SVR, VCR, and VCR-LP recordings are all mutually incompatible.

SVR system met with a cool response in Britain and most of Europe, outside Germany. The system was only marketed for about a year and now, like VCR-LP, is obsolete. Remainder stock of both systems may still be found in some shops dotted around the country, usually heavily discounted and both

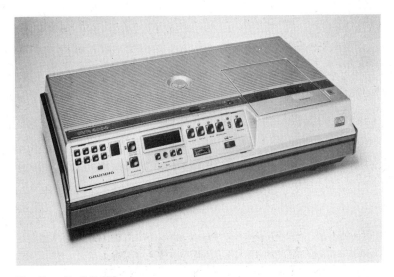

The Grundig SVR4004

companies claim that spares and tapes are still available. However, both companies have turned their attention on the allegedly co-developed Video 2000 system.

Video 2000

The result of many years research, the Video 2000 format has suffered crippling delays and technical difficulties since its official announcement in 1979. The format, a cassette slightly smaller than a VHS tape but larger than a Betamax, is radically different from any other in that tapes may be turned over at the end of recording and new one started on the other 'side'. This is made possible partly by using a special formulation on Video 2000 4 hr-per-side tapes, but mainly by a control system called Dynamic Track Following, which relies on a sophisticated sequence of tape pulse codes during recording to ensure that heads read their correct track on the tape. Each 'side' takes up half the width of the ½ in tape and the format incorporates a unique 'cue track'. This is not being used at the time of writing but could serve bilingual, editing, or tape code indexing requirements. Because of dynamic track following, a 'sync' track – the string of pulses recorded along the top edge of the

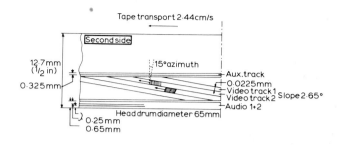

The Video 2000 recording format and two machines using the
system, the Grundig Video 2×4 Super and the Philips VR2022

tape for picture control on all other helical scan machines – is not required. Mono or stereo sound is recorded conventionally along the bottom edge of the tape.

It was Grundig's Video 2000 format recorder – the Video 2 × 4 – which eventually reached the shops first in autumn 1980. This was criticised for lack of features (still frame, double speed play, cue and review etc) given the standard of its VHS and Betamax contemporaries and for its irritating refusal to display a 'monitor' signal (the station selected on its tuner) without the tape laced up and the head drum whirring round. This engineering inelegance was dwarfed when Philips' first Video 2000 machine – the VR2020 – reached the market later that year after a tiresome succession of delays. It was discovered that the sound head was in a different position in the tape path relative to the Grundig V2 × 4, so that the soundtrack on a Grundig recording would be out of step with vision when played on a Philips machine and vice versa. The 2.5 mm error in relative position was corrected on subsequent models by shifting the sound head on each machine 1.25 mm to a common position.

LVR

LVR, or Linear Video Recording, has been mooted and promised for a long time in recent years. The idea is based, however, on the early attempts of the BBC to capture video signals on magnetic tape with its cumbersome VERA machine.

Instead of spinning heads at high speeds against a slow-moving tape, LVR returns to the original idea of keeping the head fixed and whizzing tape past it at high speed. What has changed is the mechanical and electronic technology to make a more compact, reliable and lower speed machine possible.

BASF was the first company to declare a hand in LVR research and still owns the initials LVR as a registered trade mark. It is now believed the company has suspended the project after many years of development. BASF's system, designed primarily for portable use, used plastic encased spools of blank tape, with the free end of the tape automatically threaded onto a resident spool within the machine. The tape was then propelled by a large drum forming a dual-capstan loop at about 4 metres per second. At the end of the tape the drum would

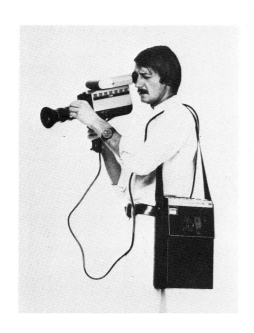

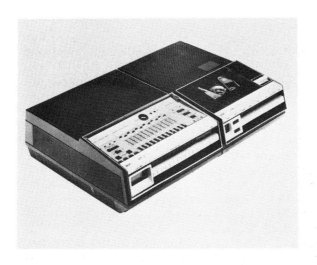

The BASF LVR portable in use with a camera and
accompanied by a tuner/timer

instantaneously reverse, and the small fixed recording head drop the depth of one track. This process was repeated from end to end until the whole width of the tape had been recorded. Video and audio signals were coded onto the same track through the single recording head. There were two erase heads, one for each direction fore and aft of the signal head.

The other company publicly admitting an LVR interest is Toshiba, whose mains-powered prototypes have been demonstrated at various exhibitions around the world including trade shows in London. Toshiba's machine uses an endless cartridge of ½ in tape in a similar fashion to the now obsolete 8-track stereo cartridge system. Specially back-lubricated tape rattles round at about 5½ metres per second and the video plus audio

The Toshiba LVR machine

signal head drops one track each time the join comes round. In this way 300 tracks are laid across the ½ in tape to give two hours of recording.

An advantage of any LVR system is its relatively small number of components and hence low weight and cost, although tape packaging is more involved than with conventional video cassettes.

The other advantage is access. To find a favourite spot on a VHS or Betamax tape you have to laboriously spool through to where you think it is, play a bit, spool some more, and so on

20

until you find the part you want. With LVR you simply skip across the tape, watching the picture as you go. You can index a sequence precisely by noting the track number; whereas the index counter on a conventional recorder only makes sense if it has been zeroed from the start, and even so is prone to errors due to tape slip. A prototype demonstrated at 1980's Chicago Consumer Electronics Show used two signal heads in tandem to replay a choice of two programmes from one tape. Toshiba also claims that multiplex stereo (as used on radio broadcasts) could be recorded on the video tape tracks.

The big unknown is whether Toshiba's LVR tapes will stand the strain of high speed, continuous loop operation, if and when the machines ever reach the marketplace.

CVC

Compact Video Cassette is the name Technicolor, Grundig and Canon are using to describe a primarily portable format developed by Funai with special tape from Fuji (both Japanese). Like the long-obsolete Akai VK portable format, it employs helically scanned ¼ in tape, but records in colour as against VK's monochrome-only capability. Another difference is the size of the cassette case, little more than that of a conventional compact audio cassette. As a result the machine is relatively lightweight and compact, with many of the basic features of its bulkier VHS and Betamax contemporaries. Maximum playing time is 30 min, which for video movie-making may well be considered adequate. The theory with this and other new portable formats is that the conventional mains machine is not replaced, but rather takes on the role of an editing machine for the rough 'takes' made on location. Commercial success for this system is difficult to predict, but initial technical results are very promising indeed.

Miniature formats

While many predicted that LVR technology held the key to portable video on a mass scale, multi-million pound research of the world's most advanced consumer electronics corporations (mostly in Japan) indicates otherwise. Despite helical

Compact Video Cassette camera and recorder

scan's relative complexity, companies are basing long-term development plans around helical machines of a refined and miniaturised design. An example is of course Technicolor's CVC. A few steps up the technological ladder is 8mm Video, a new standard agreed by Sony, Hitachi, Philips and Panasonic, among others. This helical scan format will be integrated into hand-held camera/video recorder combination units in the mid-80s.

Conventional portable recording kits of today – including CVC – comprise a video recorder (usually shoulder-mounted) and a hand-held or shoulder-resting camera containing one or more image-resolving 'tubes'. These tubes contain light-sensitive elements which register the brilliance of television's three component colours – red, green and blue – in a single tube (on cheap cameras) or three separate tubes (on profes-sional cameras). Some intermediately priced cameras measure two colours in two tubes and derive the third (usually green). Either way, tube cameras operate by scanning the picture elements with electrons and measuring the charge picked up on those elements. Where light exists the charge is high; where no light exists the charge is low. In this way the picture is built up, using what is essentially a valve technology. Camera tubes are bulky and need very expensive coatings to produce sensitive, good quality performance.

But the new combined camera-recorders use a solid state charge-coupled device (CCD) to resolve the picture. These do not need electronic scanning as they deliver a sequence of picture information direct and are consequently very compact.

The Sony Video Movie – first camera/recorder prototype

In short, CCDs make the idea of a combined camera-recorder possible. Sony was the first to announce designs for such a unit which it called the Video Movie in late 1980. Hitachi followed shortly afterwards with a design called Mag-Camera, which is incompatible with Video Movie. Then came Micro Video

The Panasonic (Matsushita) Micro Video System also uses a microcassette

System (Panasonic), followed by Handy Video (Sanyo). All used miniature helical scan recorders integrated with the CCD camera and lens assemblies. These companies have now agreed to standardise with 8mm Video.

VHS

Introduced: 1978
Inventor: Victor Corporation of Japan (JVC)
Cassette size: 156 × 96 × 25mm (width × height × depth)
Maximum tape duration: 4 hours
Tape: ½in chromium dioxide (BASF), cobalt-doped ferric oxide (Fuji, TDK, 3M by different process), or mixture of both

24

Video writing speed: 4.83 metres per second
Top machine features: Speed play, slow motion, frame-by-frame, still frame, cue & review, tape indexing (pulses on tape), auto-rewind, remote control, remote programming. Timer: 8 events over 14 days. Dolby noise reduction
Future potential: Soundtrack can be split to permit stereo or bilingual operation

Betamax

Introduced: 1978
Inventor: Sony Corporation of Japan
Cassette size: 104 × 88 × 25 mm (WHD)
Maximum tape duration: 3¼ hours
Tape: ½ in chromium dioxide, cobalt-doped ferric oxide, or mixture of both (Sony)
Tape speed: 18.73 mm per second
Video writing speed: 6.6 metres per second
Top machine features: Speed play, slow motion, frame-by-frame, still frame, cue & review, tape indexing (pulses on tape), auto-rewind, remote control. Timer: 4 events over 14 days. Tape auto-changer on C7 Sony model. Dolby noise reduction
Future potential: Soundtrack can be split to permit stereo or bilingual operation

Video 2000

Introduced: 1980
Inventor: Philips Industries Ltd
Cassette size: 189 × 109 × 25 mm (WHD)
Maximum tape duration: 4 hours each side
Tape: ½ in chromium dioxide, cobalt-doped ferric oxide, or mixture of both
Tape speed: 24.4 mm per second
Video writing speed: 5.08 metres per second
Top machine features: Speed play, slow motion, frame-by-frame, still frame, cue and review, 'go to' indexing (tape counter readings), auto rewind, optional remote control. Timer: All machines are multi-event, typically 5 events over 16 days. Own system of noise reduction
Future potential: Auto-reverse at end of each side claimed a possibility. Cue track incorporated for stereo, bilingual, or time-coded operation

VCR-LP

Introduced: 1977 (Long Play version)
Inventor: Philips Industries Ltd
Cassette size: 145 × 127 × 41 mm (WHD)
Maximum tape duration: 3 hours
Tape: ½ in chromium dioxide, cobalt-doped ferric oxide, or mixture of both
Tape speed: 65.5 mm per second
Video writing speed: 8.1 metres per second
Top machine features: None of the above. Timer: 1 event over 10 days
Future potential: Obsolete format, though many still in circulation. Tapes still being produced; spares have been stockpiled. Superseded by Philips Video 2000 system

3

Video in the home

While old wives' tales seem to have as much influence in this technological age as they did four centuries ago, the practicalities of video – and indeed the very concept of recording pictures on tape – are better understood today, broadly speaking, than they have ever been. Misconceptions do still persist however. There are still those who ask where to get their video tapes processed; whether a special adaptor is

Custom-built furniture houses the TV and the video recorder and keeps it clean and out of sight until needed. A number of such cabinets are available in different styles

27

needed; or even where a videotape should be inserted in their television set! More enlightened queries include how much power the recorder consumes, and whether the video recorder affects everyday viewing.

The first thing to make clear is that you do not need a specially adapted television set to use a video recorder. Most modern 625-line sets are suitable, and it does not matter whether it is a black and white or a colour model. Some older televisions are intolerant of the relatively sloppy way a video

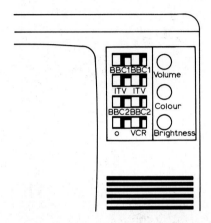

On modern televisions there is a channel specifically marked for use with a video recorder. The actual letters used may vary from one maker to another

recorder presents its pictures. Broadcasts contain a regular chain of control pulses which video recorders tend to present in a less regular stream. The key lies in what engineers describe as the 'timebase' of the television's tuner. Some televisions have a selector button marked 'AV', or 'VR' or 'VTR' designed for video recorder signals. Others accept video machines on all buttons. Your dealer can advise on your particular television's suitability for video replay. Secondly, in no way does a video recorder damage your set or affect your normal television viewing. You do not need a special aerial – nor any tools, oils, greases or cleaning fluids. As you need is somewhere to put the recorder and a ready supply of tapes.

Checking the aerial signal

Basically, if you can receive reasonable quality pictures with your aerial plugged straight into the television set, you will get reasonable results with a video recorder. Most people want their television signal to be of a high quality, however, given the degradation which occurs in any recording process and that the programmes recorded are those which the user wants to see at their best.

For best results you need a well made UHF (ultra high frequency) aerial, accurately pointed at your strongest local television transmitter. If you live in a weak signal area, you may

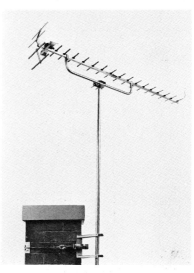

A medium/long range UHF aerial by Antiference, with a gain of just under 15 dB (about ×5)

A high gain aerial from Antiference with a gain of about 18 dB (about ×8) and very good directional properties

need a special aerial or even a booster amplifier. If on the other hand your house is practically next door to a transmitter, or the signal is otherwise very strong, you may need to use an attenuator. This is a small barrel about the size of a coaxial plug which fits between the aerial plug and socket. They are

PLUG   SOCKET

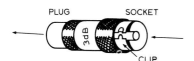

CLIP

An in-line attenuator inserted in the aerial lead prevents overloading in areas of high field strength. Values from 3 dB (÷2) up to 24 d B (÷300) are available

29

calibrated according to attenuation: 3 dB, 6 dB, 10 dB and so on up to 24 dB. Advice, and the necessary equipment, is available from any reputable aerial contractor.

Connecting to the television

The aerial is connected straight to the video recorder, and a coaxial lead connects the recorder to the television. This should clarify one of the biggest myths surrounding video. When you are recording a television programme, you are not recording from the television set; you are recording straight from the aerial.

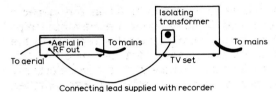

Connecting the video recorder to the TV

The lead connecting recorder to television is of ordinary coaxial cable – but it is protected against an electrical fault occurring in the recorder, i.e. the one supplied with the machine. The recorder is quite independent of the television. The television is purely a means of replaying pictures and sound – just as it is normally with broadcast programmes. The video recorder is tuned to stations as though it were another television set. It does not matter what station the television is tuned to, whether it is switched on or off, or whether it has a brick through the screen. The video machine records which-ever channel it has been tuned to, irrespective of the television. Although there seems little point, were you to replay tapes while the television was switched off you would not be damaging the tape, the recording on the tape, the recorder itself, or the television.

Connecting to the mains

Video recorders plug straight into an electrical socket and the power is left on all the time. Some people are alarmed at this, or rather the prospect of an electrical fault in the recorder starting a fire. There is nothing wrong with such caution in general but in the case of a video recorder, such fears are misplaced. The machine is thoroughly fused and, perhaps more important, consumes only a tiny amount of electricity.

A 3A fuse must be fitted to the power plug. 13A plugs are usually supplied with a 13A fuse – this should be changed before use

This is because the only components active in the machine while it is in this so-called 'standby' mode are the micro-chips and diodes which make up the digital clock – even when the timer is set to record a programme. Heat dissipated by this section is negligible – in fact the whole unit uses less electricity and gives off less heat than a conventional electric kitchen clock. When in full operation – that is, while recording or playing back TV programmes – a video recorder uses about the same amount of electricity as a living room light. The plug on all recorders should therefore be fitted with a 3A fuse.

Tuning in

Each television station puts its pictures onto what is called a carrier frequency in order to transmit. As its name suggests, a carrier frequency's job is to carry – in this case a television picture. Each television station has been given its own particular carrier frequency so that the viewer can 'tune' to the station of his choice. A video recorder must be similarly tuned in, but before this can be done it must be sending a signal down the lead which connects it to the television. Otherwise it would be like trying to tune in BBC1 (or any other station) when no programmes are being transmitted. One way of doing this is to play back a recorded cassette in the recorder and tune it into a free channel on the television as you would tune for normal television stations. If you have just bought a video recorder, however, you will hardly be likely to have a recorded cassette to hand. Most modern recorders are now fitted with a *TEST* or

CH. SET switch which provides a simple pattern signal to tune to on the television. Many still do rely on the recorded cassette method, however, so check that the dealer provides such a cassette before you purchase.

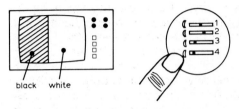

black   white

Tune the TV until a perfect test pattern is reproduced from the recorder. If no 'Test' or 'Ch. Set.' rear panel switch is provided, tune to a pre-recorded cassette

Video recorders have completely independent tuners of their own so that they can record a different channel to the one the television may be tuned to. Some video machine tuners are automatic – scanning the waveband for stations and stopping when one is found – but the majority are manual. A series of thumb-wheel switches correspond to a row of front-panel channel selector buttons. To prepare this section to receive broadcasts and make television recording possible use the same method as you would to tune a normal television.

Firstly, the television must be tuned to the recorder in the way described earlier. Next you select 'record' on older video machines, in order to monitor the recorder's tuner section (modern machines return you to the tuner in all modes except 'play'). A video recorder does not affect your normal television viewing in any way. All television channels pass through the recorder and are not affected on a properly aligned machine. Watching the same channel on television while it is being recorded does not weaken or degenerate the recorded picture.

The right environment

Considering their complexity, video recorders are pretty robust machines. Yet some people fear that a video recorder may be too delicate for use in a family home with children, pets and all. In fact all the machines available at the moment have been specially designed for foolproof service. For example, all the operating controls are linked by an interlock system which is superior to all but the most expensive audio tape cassette decks. This simply means that you cannot – without a good deal of difficulty – switch direct from rewind to play (as an example) without giving the machine time to stop the tape and prepare for the next mode in the correct way. Also a video recorder's casing is scratch resistant and contains no easily damaged wooden parts and the operation switches are generally more robust than on many pieces of hi-fi equipment. As for aesthetics, you may either decide that video recorders are fairly sleek, elegant or whatever – or that one lump of equipment is about as ugly as any other.

There are some general points to be borne in mind when installing and using a video recorder. The machine should stand away from the carpet, where there are always small particles of dust, to reduce the risk of debris being drawn up by thermal currents into the mechanism of the recorder. In fact an adequate space should always be left both above and below the machine for ventilation currents to circulate – certain parts of the machine become quite warm in use. By the same token, video recorders do not like dusty or humid conditions – like kitchens, workshops and garages. Do not position the recorder too close to your television set or you could suffer 'herringbone' interference patterns on the screen.

It is also unwise to bring a machine in from the cold into a warm room and operate it immediately. As you know, a cold object (especially a metal one) brought into a warm atmosphere attracts condensation. In the case of a video recorder, minute droplets of water form on the largest metal components; typically the head drum and certain guide posts. If the machine is operated in this condition the moisture encourages the tape to stick to the rotating drum with possibly disastrous results. Certainly the tape would be creased or even snapped but worse still is the chance of damage to the delicate and expensive video heads.

Portable recorders are frequently moved around from cold to warm surroundings and for this reason are all fitted with 'dew' or 'wet' indicators to warn the operator. Several have miniature heaters built into the head drum to return to normal working as soon as possible. These refinements are not generally incorporated in mains operated equipment.

Ready for recording

Assuming that the recorder is connected up, tuned in, and sitting comfortably, you are now ready to make a recording. Make sure that any plastic stickers have been peeled from the cassette carrier and front panels, and that any cardboard packing has been removed from the carrier. The tape cassette must be inserted according to the instructions normally printed on the casing : label uppermost, tape side first.

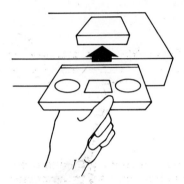

Insert the cassette firmly, label uppermost, tape side first

Cassette carriers of the pop-up type must be firmly pushed down and 'record' selected in accordance with the recorder handbook. Do a short recording first to check that the system is working correctly. If it is not, be sure to refer to the handbook first before concluding that something is faulty. Around nine out of ten calls received by dealers from distressed video users are prompted by what turns out to be an operator error. While many instruction handbooks leave a lot to be desired, most people barely glance at them, and not surprisingly, get things wrong. You must operate the machine to a script until you get to know the routines instinctively.

Using the timer

The most modern machines have quite complex timers capable of remembering several instructions to record. These are called 'programmable' because you can programme a series of recording 'events', each with their own details of channel, start time, finish time (or duration), day, and even week number in certain cases.

A timer can only work properly if it is set to the right time of day in the first place. It is best to synchronise a timer to the speaking clock on the telephone or Greenwich 'pips' on the radio. Radio 4 (UK) is best for this, broadcasting time signals at 8am, 1pm and 6pm. Select the time to be synchronised on the timer clock, and hold the 'clock set' or 'clock adj' button in until the final pip or stroke (telephone) is sounded. In the case of 12-hour clocks where *am* and *pm* are indicated, be sure to set the correct period of the day when setting the clock, and in subsequent timed programmes.

"On the third stroke, it will be 1 o'clock precisely"   "Pip, pip ...."   ".... pip"

Setting the clock display

Broadcast schedules are notorious for running behind time. So when setting 'switch off' or 'duration' time for programmes always add on about five minutes to allow for late running – more if the programme follows a sports or other live event. There is nothing more frustrating than missing the very end of a recorded programme. Single-event timers, as found on early and cheaper machines, are fairly foolproof once you get to learn the sequence.

Mistakes are mostly made not in the setting up of a recording event on the timer, but more frequently in the priming of recorder controls for that event. The power switch is commonly left in 'operate' or switched to 'off' instead of 'timer'. On so-called 'mechanical' decks, where the tape transport is activated by deep-throw switches instead of electrical touch-buttons, operators forget to engage 'record'. Many more forget to check the tuner buttons and end up recording unwanted material from another television channel. The answer is to establish a routine with the instruction book and rigorously check it before going off to do something else.

The programmable timer offers far more opportunity to the error-prone operator. There are many more details to pro-gramme and check, with the added possibility of setting recording events which clash with one another. The best way to feed these mini-computers with the facts and figures of your viewing whims is to begin by writing everything down. Find out the order in which the timer accepts information (from the recorder handbook), and write down your sequence of events in that order. You can see whether programmes conflict before even attempting to set the timer and the list is useful for checking everything afterwards.

The sophisticated 'chips' or LSICs (Large Scale Integrated Circuits) developed for programmable timers usually deal with conflicting programmes in one of two ways. One type flashes the programme entered first on and off (e.g. the Panasonic NV-7000). The other gives priority to the programme starting first (JVC HR-7700, Ferguson 3V23, both made by JVC). The first method is arguably more useful; but with a logical list of programmes written down, the situation should not arise. A final point about programmable operation. Be sure to keep the recorder well supplied with tapes. These machines accept anything up to eight recording events and you need to regularly insert fresh blank tapes to catch all of these.

Finding a favourite sequence

As tape lengths get longer – Video 2000 and the latest VHS tapes both offer four hours continuous recording – the need for some method of indexing recordings increases. Manufacturers have responded with two methods of 'labelling' positions on the cassette – mechanical counters and tape pulsing.

Mechanical counters are normally connected to the right hand (take-up) spool. By taking note of counter readings at important points, a crude index can be made for the tape. I say crude because this method is subject to a number of error-producing factors. One is the tape tension in the so-called 'pancake' of tape wound onto the take-up spool, which can vary according to whether the tape has been fast wound or played up to the index point. This is commonly called tape-slip error.

Another flaw of the mechanical system is its non-linearity. At the beginning of a tape, the take-up spool has a small outside diameter and so turns quite fast. Consequently the counter turns relatively quickly, and because the number of digits changing per minute is high, the accuracy is reasonably good.

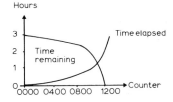

Hours

Simple graph relating counter readings to time elapsed and remaining. This must be derived by logging readings at intervals throughout a standard tape. With thinner (long play) tapes, a new table is required

Tape slip error is practically negligible because the pancake is very small. Towards the end of the tape, however, the take-up spool (and so the counter) moves very slowly. Needless to say, tape-slip error is at a peak because most of the tape has been wound onto the take-up spool. By starting from zero and logging the counter of intervals throughout a tape, a rough guide to time elapsed or remaining can be drawn up (see diagram).

So, the accuracy of mechanical counters goes from reasonable to awful between the beginning and end of the tape, as digits correspond to progressively less tape (and hence time). The final drawback is that such counters only make sense if they are set to zero at the beginning of each cassette.

Despite these shortcomings, Philips has based its indexing system on the mechanical counter. Video 2000 format recorders have a 'GO TO' function where you can enter a given index number and the machine automatically winds or rewinds to find it. The counter is zeroed automatically whenever a new tape is inserted.

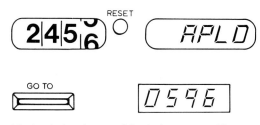

Mechanical and tape pulsing index systems. The familiar mechanical type (top left) is driven by the take-up spool, as with audio equipment. Sharp's APLD (Automatic Programme Locate Device) (top right) can count magnetic pulses inserted on the tape at the start of recordings. Video 2000 'Go To' facility (bottom) remembers mechanical tape counter numbers, displayed electronically

A better method is tape pulsing. This involves a low frequency tone, inaudible during normal play, being superimposed on the soundtrack at the beginning of each recording. During winding modes, the tone is easily identified from the high frequency babble of the soundtrack and can be used as a signal to stop the tape. Apart from errors arising from the time taken to stop the tape – which are tiny compared to the mechanical system – this method is consistently accurate and does not depend on starting from the beginning of the tape, once you know roughly where you are.

Several VHS and Betamax manufacturers now incorporate the tape pulse system, but Sharp has devised a particularly useful refinement called APLD (Automatic Programme Locate Device). Here you can instruct the machine to count forwards or backwards to any one of the pulses on the tape. During subsequent wind or rewind, APLD electronics count each pulse as it passes until the necessary total is reached and the tape is stopped ready for playback. Some machines include a manual pulsing switch for indexing your own points of interest on the tape.

The simplest form of index relies on the mechanical counter but is nevertheless very useful. It is called 'zero stop memory' and is a feature of practically all home video recorders. If you press the button marked 'memory', the machine disengages from rewind mode (in some cases from wind also) when it encounters 999 on the tape counter. In this way you can use tape counter zero as a temporary marker for the start of a recording (or any other point of interest on the tape).

Protecting recordings from erasure

All home video cassettes have some protective system of preventing unintentional recording on the tape. This usually takes the form of a thin plastic 'lug' at the back which can be snapped off to protect the cassette, similar to those found on compact audio cassettes. Should you decide to record over the programmes after all, you can quite easily stick a strip of adhesive tape across the 'hole' once occupied by the lug.

Philips, however, uses a type of selector switch on its Video 2000 cassettes which can be moved from 'normal' to 'record disable' positions at will. There are two such switches – one for each side of the tape – at the rear corners of the cassette.

Removable lugs to protect recordings against erasure: top left, on a VHS cassette; top right, on a Betamax cassette. The picture at bottom left shows the protective selector switches on a Video 2000 cassette

In each case, a small sensor rod approaches the lug (or hole in the case of Video 2000) on the cassette when 'record' is selected. If an obstruction is encountered, recording carries on as normal. If the rod is able to travel without resistance, however, a switch is thrown which inhibits the record mode and the record switch (on mechanical type machines) does not engage or the record indicator (on electrical touch-button machines) does not light. These systems provide a worthwhile protection against inadvertent erasure and should be made use of on treasured recordings.

Sound through your hi-fi

One of the bonuses of using a video recorder, in the case of all VHS and Betamax machines (and optional on Philips and Grundig), is the facility to feed high quality television sound through a hi-fi amplifier. By connecting 'audio out' from the

39

recorder to the 'aux' or 'tape' input of your hi-fi amplifier, you can enjoy a sound quality many times better than that of the average television set (in mono of course).

This is particularly so when you use the recorder to 'monitor' a programme rather than listening to one off-tape. (On older machines you must press 'record' to achieve this; but modern machines return you to the tuner in all modes except 'play'.) Television sound is broadcast on a VHF subcarrier and so the quality is comparable to VHF (FM) radio.

Whether that quality is passed on depends very much on the pedigree of your recorder's tuner. If this aspect appeals to you, insist on hearing sound through a hi-fi amplifier before buying. Listen for a general buzz (bad alignment of sound subcarrier frequency), interference from the visual signal particularly when captions or strong colours appear (cheap system of sound decoding) or background hiss (cheap/unstable components in the sound chain).

You will never achieve the same quality from sound coming off videotape as with 'live' television because of the host of inadequacies associated with sound recording on home video equipment, although Dolby noise reduction on some machines has improved this.

Replacing the soundtrack

The process works the other way around too. You can record your own sound onto a videotape with most machines by connecting 'rec o/p' or 'to tape' outputs on your hi-fi amplifier to 'audio in' on the recorder and selecting 'audio dub', if fitted (see *Copying and Editing Recordings*). Of course you have no control over the sound level on the recorder – this is adjusted automatically. You can monitor the sound through the television – just select the video recorder channel, press 'audio dub', and listen. It is wise to engage 'pause' while you are checking that everything is working satisfactorily. The sound may be distorted, this means the amplifier output is too strong for the automatic gain control in the recorder. You need to attenuate the hi-fi amplifier's output. This can be done with an in-line attenuator (available from good hi-fi component shops), by turning down the source (in the case of a tuner or tape recorder), selecting 'low output' on the amplifier recording socket switch (if fitted), or by incorporating a sound mixer (available from larger hi-fi stores) which must operate to a 'line

40

level' output. Be warned that cheaper battery-powered mixers normally operate at microphone level, which is far too low, and only accept microphone inputs.

All connections to and from a hi-fi amplifier are made with ordinary screened cable. The sockets on the recorder will be of the phono or DIN type, depending on the model. Where a DIN socket is used, inputs and outputs are combined in the one socket, on separate pins as defined by the DIN standard. The necessary leads can be bought off the shelf – if you do not want to make up your own – from good hi-fi accessory shops.

Video head cleaning

As a general rule, you should not attempt to clean video heads yourself, but you may have come across some of these so-called 'video head cleaning cassettes'. There are basically two categories: The 'dry' type containing plastic tape with a moderately abrasive coating; and the 'wet' type containing a lint material impregnated typically with methylated spirits. I have always been sceptical of these products but to assess their long-term good or evil is rather difficult – and potentially expensive.

In 1980 VHS manufacturers issued a joint statement to the UK press broadly announcing that such devices did not carry their approval. The statement went on to say that 'dry' cleaning cassettes were considered relatively harmless but at the same time ineffective. The 'wet' type was more forcefully condemned. The spirit contained a dye which could be left behind in the tape path, and more specifically, on the heads. Neither cassette attacked the areas where a build-up of shed oxide can occur – that is, either side of the slightly protruding heads on the head drum circumference. Helical scanning is an inherently abrasive process. Cleaning tapes follow the same route as regular tape and do not radically improve on the normal self-cleaning action of the system. So if you suspect your heads are dirty, or rather that tape to head contact is being impaired by oxide build-up either side of the head (characterised by a 'snowy' picture, assuming that reception was good during recording), ask your dealer to inspect the heads and if necessary to tackle the extremely critical job of removing the debris with solvent. This may sound easy, but a few wipes across the head with an oxide-contaminated cleaning stick could seriously damage the head.

Signal splitting

To feed more than one television from a video recorder, for example a second television in the bedroom or kitchen, a signal splitter of some kind must be used. Simply joining television cable together is unsatisfactory because the impedance (AC resistance) of a television system must be a certain value – typically 75 ohms – which would be modified by crude cable-joining.

Splitters come in two varieties – active and passive. Active splitters incorporate a signal amplifier and usually need an external power source. They are generally only required for more than two or three 'splits' and need careful alignment of input and output levels in order to function correctly. More common is the passive type, which uses no power and normally consists of only a few resistors.

The most usual requirement is for a two-way passive splitter. These are available from aerial dealers, or can be constructed in a screened enclosure yourself. The diagram shows the configuration of three 27 ohm resistors to split a single output

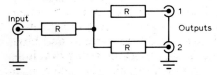

A simple passive splitter using three 27 ohm resistors, R

(e.g. the video recorder) into two television inputs. All connections must be made with the correct UHF connectors and cable. If you are splitting an aerial signal – for feeding two television sets or a VTR/TV and secondary TV – you must be sure that the aerial is picking up an adequate signal. This type of splitter cuts the signal into two outputs, each at half the original strength (a reduction of 3 dB).

Video recorder outputs do not suffer in the same way since recordings are made at an optimum level, by amplifying the aerial signal if necessary. So you can usually better afford a signal reduction to the recorder output than the aerial, unless you live in a high signal-strength area (see *Checking the aerial signal*). If you are in any doubt, see your local aerial dealer who should understand the complexities involved in relation to local television reception conditions.

4

How video works

A video recorder can be likened to a television set without a screen. In other words, it contains all the electronics necessary to interpret a television broadcast, but instead of displaying it on a screen it puts the picture on tape. This sounds like a remarkable achievement. To appreciate this technological miracle, however, it is necessary to know how television itself works.

A television picture is produced by dividing an image into 625 horizontal lines. These lines are further split into small horizontal units or 'dots'. Each dot is given a certain brilliance value by the camera, which assesses the red, green and blue components in the image. This is a complicated string of values in itself, but of course movement must also be taken into account. So 25 picture 'frames' are produced every second, each composed of 625 lines of dot information.

Each frame contains two 'fields' of lines. One field provides even lines to the screen, the other odd lines. The technique is known as interlace scanning. Lines are scanned across the screen from left to right, one at a time, from top to bottom. The two fields are simply components of the complete frame; there

Schematic diagram of how a TV picture is made up. Odd and even sets of lines (fields) are interlaced sequentially to produce 25 full frames each second

is no difference in action between them. So why split frames into two fields? The reason is to reduce flicker. If a complete frame was generated every $\frac{1}{25}$ sec, the eye would unconsciously see top lines fading by the time lines were scanned at the bottom of the screen and a flicker effect would result. This could of course be reduced by increasing the image-retention of the television's phosphor coating but this would smudge action. Alternatively whole frames could be replaced every $\frac{1}{50}$ sec, which is how often fields are replaced in our system today (to synchronise with the mains frequency of 50 Hz), as described. This, would, however, increase the rate of information flow to unmanageable proportions. So like any technical system, television picture generation is a compromise – but a very good one.

With a little effort, most people can grasp the principle of television picture construction. What they cannot understand is how all the light and shade, colour, action, and sound can travel down a single aerial wire and make any sort of sense at the other end. The secret of television is information in sequence, which is logical when you recall the way frames are written onto the screen. Details of, for example, the colour and brilliance of the very first line on the television screen are established by the studio camera just as your television is scanning that same line at home. The operation is kept in step partly by synchronising everything to the mains frequency and also by special check pulses inserted at the end of each line, field and frame.

All this represents a good deal of information being passed on in a short period of time. The only way to achieve such a high rate of information flow electrically is to use very high frequencies or alternations of voltage. Whereas the highest pitch of sound that we can hear vibrates at around 20 000 hertz (named after the 19th century physicist Heinrich Hertz), colour television transmission requires several *million* hertz.

So all the components of a television picture can be made to travel down a cable by observing a carefully timed sequence. Sound incidentally is specially coded to travel with the picture by a process which involves those vital ingredients of television distribution: radio frequency carriers.

Radio frequency carriers – television's messengers

Radio frequency (RF) carriers do precisely what their name suggests – carry radio frequencies. They make the whole idea of transmitting radio and television 'over the air' possible.

So what exactly are they? Why are they so important? In colour television, an RF carrier is simply an ultra-high frequency onto which the 'raw' video output and sound of a television studio is superimposed. This is because if the basic picture signals were fed to a transmitter, they would travel only a very short distance. By superimposing those signals onto a frequency which can travel for many miles, the picture details get a 'piggy back' delivery to an enormously bigger area. The process used in television is called 'frequency modulation' (FM), the same as that used on better quality radio broadcasts. Once superimposed on an RF carrier in this way, a video signal is referred to as 'encoded'.

Video and sound signals are superimposed onto an ultra-high frequency carrier by a process called 'frequency modulation' (FM). This schematic shows the basic principle of RF encoding. Upon reception the UHF carrier is removed by a tuned circuit to leave the original signals

The advantages are obvious – better distribution, and better quality of reception. All you need is a 'decoder' in the television receiver to remove the RF carrier and you neatly have the original signal just as it left the studio. By arranging for different television stations to use different carrier frequencies, you can allow the viewer to 'tune' between stations. This is how television distribution works today, throughout the world.

Every home video recorder has a 'decoder' section – more commonly known as a tuner – which is set up to receive the various television stations in the same way as the push-button tuner on a modern television set. The 'raw' video is then prepared for recording onto tape and the sound separated for recording on the videotape soundtrack. To replay a recording through a normal television set, it is necessary to 'encode' the signals once again. The recorder superimposes the picture and sound onto another carrier, different from that of any of the television stations, so that its signal can be independently tuned on the television set (see also *Video in the home*).

Replaying a videotape involves some unnecessary processing. The signal from the tape is encoded, passes about 2 metres down a connecting lead into the television and is then decoded before ultimately appearing on the screen. Clearly the encode/decode conversions are somewhat inelegant but unless you have a television monitor – one which accepts a plain video input with separate sound – these quality-degrading conversions have to be tolerated. Almost all video recorders are equipped with video and sound terminals for use with a television monitor. These become useful when making copies of videotapes and listening through a hi-fi amplifier (see Chapter 3). If you do want to obviate the encode/decode sequence and watch plain video, get a receiver/monitor television. A television monitor alone cannot accept normal television broadcasts – except via the VTR – as it has no tuner section.

It may already be clear that a videotape recording contains no RF carrier components. This is fortunate as the relationship between picture and sound carriers used in the UK and Northern Ireland, for example, is unique. As things stand, however, a tape recorded in Britain is compatible with any other PAL country (assuming the format is the same of course) except Brazil.

Recording pictures on tape

So far the principles of television operation have been established up to, but not including, its recording on tape. Now we can look at the remarkable way in which television's transient images can be captured on videotape. Firstly, let us look at the process of magnetic recording.

In the nineteenth century, the British scientist Michael Faraday established the mysterious relationship between magnetism and electricity. He observed that an electrical current flowing through a wire produced a tiny magnetic field around the wire. When a coil of wire was subjected to a changing magnetic field – a strong magnet moving across the coil – a current flowed in the wire. Faraday went on to quantify the relationship with detailed research.

His discoveries were to prompt the most significant inventions of the industrial revolution in Victorian times: the generator, converting mechanical force into electricity and the electric motor, converting electricity into mechanical force.

In 1900 a Danish scientist, Valdemar Poulsen, succeeded in exploring Faraday's basic principles to store information – namely the human voice. It had already been established that soft iron was very good at retaining induced magnetism. Poulsen reasoned that by magnetising a strip of iron according to a changing electrical sequence, he could then play the sequence back by running the system in reverse. His historic voice experiment involved 'recording' an electrical sequence generated by a microphone (itself an electromagnetic device) onto iron wire passing an electromagnet between two very large spools.

Poulsen's recordings could be 'erased' by using a strong, fixed magnet to re-orientate the wire's magnetic patterns into a jumble of relative silence. Edison's phonograph – the forerunner of today's LP record player – was superior to Poulsen's system in terms of quality, convenience (the wire method was not only cumbersome but also dangerous) and relatively low background noise.

With the development of paper-backed, and later, plastic-backed, magnetic iron oxide tape in the early 1950s, the magnetic recording medium – which was of course re-usable and could now be edited easily – was to become established. Very soon after television developed, video became the next target for the new magnetic medium. Various formats were developed (see *Video Formats*) until the invention of the helical scan principle on which all home video recorders operate.

So how do these whirring bundles of machinery manage to produce a good quality picture on magnetic tape? The basic principle is no more than a variation of the well-established technique of recording information on tape, pioneered on audio machines. Most of the signal electronics are standard television circuits. The most demanding requirements are accurate speed control and precise mechanical engineering, both essential for the theory to work. A lot of research has gone into developing large scale integrated circuits (LSICs) for integrated tape control, transport logic and timer functions.

Today's helical scan recorders have two video heads diametrically opposed on a rotating drum. Tape is wrapped around just over half of the drum's circumference so that one of the heads is always in contact with the tape. Each head handles one field, so that after two revolutions a whole television frame is completed. The head drum, which must rotate at 1500 rpm to produce 25 frames each second, is tilted relative to the tape's motion so that each head starts scanning from one side of the tape and describes a diagonal track across the tape width.

Tape speed and the tracking control

Along the bottom edge of the tape on all formats except Video 2000 is a so-called sync track, which is recorded as a train of 25 Hz pulses to ensure that the tape is replayed at the correct speed by the correct head. Also, at the end of each video track a short burst of check pulses is recorded. This tells the recorder, again on playback, whether the head drum is rotating at the correct speed to achieve synchronisation with the television set.

The sync track and video check pulses are fed back through servo electronics to contribute to an overall control system, which often includes a crystal/tachometer servo on the capstan. The control system is responsible for checking that the

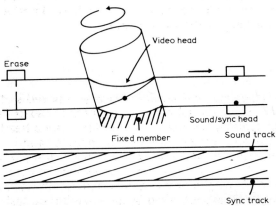

Tape is scanned in a helical configuration by diametrically opposed video heads mounted on a rotating drum (top). Sound and sync tracks are recorded by a twin-gap stationary head on the take-up side of the head drum. Machines with 'audio dub' facility use a twin-gap erase head to allow erasure of the sound track only. The bottom diagram shows linear video tape tracks viewed flat (you cannot actually see these on the tape). Each video track contains one TV field. Two consecutive fields make one complete TV frame. The Philips Video 2000 system uses half the width to permit recording on both 'sides' of the tape (see *Video formats*)

48

tape is replayed at the same speed as it was recorded, that each head reads its correct track, and making corrections to capstan speed, head drum speed, or sometimes both. The 'tracking' control fitted to all machines except those of the Video 2000

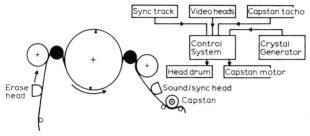

Simplified tape path of a VHS recorder and associated control system

format increases the scope of the capstan speed variation to accommodate any relatively large difference in playing speed encountered on a 'foreign' recorded tape, which would otherwise cause mistracking by the video heads.

Video heads

The tiny video heads are set into diametrically opposed slots on the circumference of the spinning section of the head drum assembly, which is finely balanced at the factory. Video heads are very delicate and should not be touched, cleaned or replaced by unskilled hands. Each head is tilted from true azimuth (where the head gap would be at a perfect right angle to its plane of motion by a few degrees, depending on the format. Because the heads are tilted by an equal but opposite amount, crosstalk – the effect when heads marginally err into adjacent tracks – is largely cancelled. This technique is called 'slant azimuth' (see *Video Formats*). Head replacement involves a dismantling of the head drum assembly and a precise lining up of the new heads – which is why it can be quite expensive (around £60-£100 on popular models). Head life varies from 1000 to 2000 hours. Any competent dealer can tell you when the heads need to be checked for wear. Never attempt any form of maintenance to the vulnerable head drum area unless you are a qualified engineer.

The soundtrack

In video recording, sound is put on a separate track on the top edge, alongside the diagonal tracks of video occupying most of the tape. A separate, stationary recording head is used, which usually incorporates a 'sync' head (for tape motion control) along the bottom edge. The exception to this is Video 2000 format, which requires no synchronisation pulses because control signals are incorporated in the video tracks (see *Dynamic Track Following*). Sound is recorded in front of its corresponding video image by a fixed amount due to the different position of sound and video heads in the tape path.

Many recorders have a split erase head to allow 'audio dubbing'. Recording is achieved by an erase head positioned in front of the video head drum and sound/sync head in the tape path. By splitting erase into two switchable gaps – one covering the video and sync tracks of the tape, the other the soundtrack – it is possible to record a new soundtrack to accompany a previously recorded video sequence. This technique is called 'audio dubbing', and is particularly useful in home video movie-making. Due to the extremely low tape speed used in home video formats (in all cases slower than a compact audio cassette), sound quality can hardly be described as hi-fi. The adjustments made to tape speed by the capstan servo can result in small but perceptible variations in sound pitch, an error referred to as wow and flutter.

More recent VHS machines incorporate the Dolby system of noise reduction familiar to hi-fi enthusiasts. Philips has its own variation of Dolby called ANR (Automatic Noise Reduction) which is fitted to Philips and Grundig Video 2000 machines.

At the time of writing, all home video recorders use an automatic gain control on soundtrack recording – there is no level control and meter system and the bias setting (switchable for different tapes on many compact audio decks), is fixed.

All video recorders except Philips have direct sound input and output sockets fitted as standard, for connection to a hi-fi amplifier or other video recorder (see *Copying and editing recordings*).

Dynamic Track Following

This is the name Philips has given to the remarkable control technique which makes its flip-over Video 2000 format possible. It is a technique, used on professional recorders but never before on a domestic machine, where each video head is mounted on a piezo-electric crystal base.

Piezo-electric crystals have the property of expanding or contracting when subjected to a voltage. This principle is exploited in quartz watches, where a voltage causes the quartz to vibrate at an accurately fixed rate. These vibrations are then

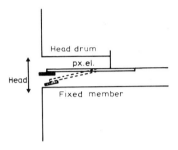

Philips' Video 2000 system incorporates Dynamic Track Following. The essence of this is a coding sequence recorded on the tape to identify each head's correct track, and piezo-electric mountings (px.el.) which can make tracking corrections by moving the heads up or down. Below: Sequence of codes superimposed onto Video 2000 video tracks. During mistracking, adjacent frequencies are read together. The resulting 'beat' frequency is used to derive a corrective piezo voltage

used as a basis for precise time measurement. The principle works in reverse too. Many lighter and gas cooker ignition systems produce their spark from the voltage produced by a 'hammered' piezo-electric crystal. The piezo-electric base is capable of shifting each head to its correct tracking position. So far, so good. But how is this achieved?

During recording, a sequence of four control frequencies are superimposed on video tracks in turn. On replay, a straying or mistracking video head reads across two adjacent video tracks and a 'beat' frequency – corresponding to the difference

51

in frequency of the superimposed control signals – is produced. This is used as a basis for a corrective control voltage fed to the piezo-electric video head base and the head is moved back in line. A relatively low frequency beat denotes an upward deviation and a high beat denotes a downward deviation. Dynamic Track Following circuitry can distinguish between the two directions of error and make the adjustment accordingly.

5

Video recorders

Home video recorders vary tremendously in complexity and price, but they all do the same basic job: record and play back television pictures and sound. Before deciding on a specific model it is important to know what facilities are available and which of these are worth paying extra for. I should stress that the best possible way to select a particular machine is to test a 'short list' of likely models in a dealer's showroom. To do this you need to be informed of the standards prevailing – or you could be sold an outdated model and miss the recorder with the right 'mix' of features, operational ease, picture quality and price to suit your needs.

Operational ease

Whatever kind of machine you choose, it must be easy for you to control and function in a way that is logical to you. Most users operate their video recorder hundreds of times during its life; if there is something awkward or clumsy about its *modus operandi* you are sure to become irritated by this over a period of time.

Ask yourself questions about certain aspects of the video recorder range before you buy. How resolute are you about format? Changing your format choice could grant access to extra features, or alternatively you may be able to buy an adequate machine at a budget price. Is front-loading for the cassette essential to you? Sacrificing this extra, where tapes are drawn in and out of a slot electronically, could save you a good deal of money. On the other hand, such a feature saves clearance space otherwise needed above the machine. Do you need easy connection for a camera or other video source (such as another machine for copying tapes)? What facilities do the machines you are looking at offer in this respect? Finally, can you understand how to operate the machine? Is it pleasing to look at, would it clutter or complement your home?

Picture quality

Modern VHS, Betamax and Video 2000 recorders perform to similar technical standards, although much depends on machine alignment. Despite Dynamic Track Following and its attendant advantages, Philips is trying to squeeze a quart out of a pint pot by recording across half the tape width of single-sided formats. Many observers argue that Video 2000 will achieve its highest standards by using metal-particle tape, with which Philips claims the format is 'upward-compatible'.

Video 2000 partners Grundig have developed the format's quality quite remarkably when 8 hr (4 hr each side) per cassette recording capacity is considered. When originally introduced the VR2020 – Philips' first Video 2000 machine – was expensive and did not have the features of its VHS and Betamax rivals. At the time of writing, both machines and tapes – including pre-recorded ones – were in good supply. Check this out with your dealer.

You can check the alignment of any recorder fairly critically by recording the BBC's *Test Card F*, which has a picture of a little girl in the middle. Check the deep colours in the picture for shift to the right (chroma delay), and blotchy patches or random snow (poor signal-to-noise ratio). Check vertical lines (of which there are plenty) for modulator ringing effects. These appear as spurious echoes to one side of the original lines. If the dealer claims this is ghosting caused by a poor aerial or the effects of a 'built-up area', adjust the tuning on the recorder with the AFC (Automatic Frequency Control) switched out. Reflected ghost images remain stationary, but ringing moves around.

Test Card F also has a series of vertical gratings to the right of the girl's picture. You can use these to check the recorder's bandwidth. The six boxes of lines correspond (from the top) to 1.5 MHz, 2.5 MHz, 3.5 MHz, 4 MHz, 4.5 MHz, and 5.25 MHz.

54

BBC Test Card F (reproduced by courtesy of the BBC)

Many television sets cannot resolve the last two or three, reproducing either a pattern of dot colours or a nondescript grey, which is quite normal.

A video recorder should have an overall bandwidth of about 3 MHz. Unfortunately this value is not on the card, but if the off-tape image is ill-defined at 2.5 MHz (second from the top), the machine is performing to a very low standard. On the other hand, a recorder resolving the 3.5 MHz grid off-tape is in extremely good condition.

An intermediate test is to flick between the original station button on the television – BBC1, BBC2, ITV etc – and check the quality against that same station tuned on the recorder, without or while recording it. Modern machines assume this 'straight-through' or 'monitor' mode in all positions except 'play' (see later). On some of the older recorders you have to select 'record' (only) to see the monitor signal. Find the station on the machine's tuner and compare television with video on the television tuner. What you are checking here is the input demodulator (tuner) and output modulator of the machine.

Weakness very often lies on the output side; you can check this subjectively by recording the test card while viewing it in monitor mode, and comparing playback. If it looks as bad but no worse than before, the main limiting factor is obviously at the output stage, not in the recording process.

Tape transport controls

The controls you will use most are those affecting the movement and manipulation of the tape. These are similar to those found on an audio cassette deck, but fall into two types: 'deep throw' mechanical, and 'touch button' electronic.

The mechanical type are the more old-fashioned, but cheaper. Tab buttons marked 'rewind', 'play', 'stop', 'wind', and so on are firmly engaged to select the various modes. Hence the expression 'deep throw', as a description of switch action. Interlock – the safety system which prevents modes being selected in conflict or in a potentially damaging sequence – is achieved mechanically. There is normally no 'transport logic' on these systems. Transport logic allows you to select the next mode without passing through 'stop' and then calculates how to make the selection.

The controls on a Sony C7 Betamax recorder

For instance, on a deep throw machine, passing direct from a winding mode to 'play' is impossible. You have to first select 'stop', then press 'play'. Likewise from 'play' to a winding mode requires you to press 'stop', waiting for the machine to unlace tape from the head drum mechanism (on VHS and Video 2000), and then selecting 'wind' or 'rewind' (more recent 'deep throw' decks obviate the waiting stage). A recorder with 'transport logic' operates a sequence which makes it possible to go from one mode to any other just by pressing a single button.

Electronic buttons rely on a microprocessor and electro-magnetic solenoid system to provide the brains and brawn to make all this possible. Any 'touch button' machine has trans-port logic built in, and usually tape motion remote control (see later) because all tape functions are switched electrically.

Ease, speed and logic – the main characteristics of electronic touch button control – are very important to some people, whereas others hardly notice the difference. Indeed, some people prefer the positive 'clunk' action of mechanical con-trols. Which type do you prefer? Find out by experiment before you choose a video system.

Picture switching

Allied to a video recorder's ability to accept and execute commands neatly and with the minimum of operator effort, is its elegance in switching inputs and outputs to suit the mode selected.

For instance, imagine yourself watching a programme re-corded in your absence on the video machine. The programme ends, and you begin rewinding the tape. At this moment, some machines would leave the screen blank. Only after you had loaded another cassette – or pressed a station button on the television – would fresh images appear. On the older machines, even to watch an ordinary television station direct would require you to move an output switch on the recorder from 'video' to 'TV'.

The most modern machines, however, – including all the 'touch button' types – show you the station tuned on the video recorder in all modes except 'play'. This is called 'automatic monitor mode' because the machine provides a monitor of the input signal whenever it is not producing a picture itself.

You may not mind switching between 'video' and 'TV' on the machine and feel that automatic monitoring of the video recorder's tuner between playbacks is unnecessary; the older machines without this facility are certainly cheaper. Alternatively, you may see it as a pleasing refinement.

One advantage of automatic monitoring, much publicised by Sony during promotion of its C7, is that on remote control recorders the facility effectively converts your receiver into a remote control television.

By switching the recorder to 'operate' but leaving the tape stationary (or even absent) with the television tuned to the recorder, you can select the programme you want to watch on the recorder's remote control. Nothing is recorded, and the machine is basically lying idle, but it does allow remote control channel selection.

The timer

The timer is what makes the popular practice of 'timeshifting' possible. It comprises a clock display showing real time, with various buttons to set the machine for recording a programme in the future.

Most timers display 24 hour time with a flashing colon between hours and minutes registering seconds. The Hitachi VT8000 series timer counts up to noon or midnight and starts another 12-hour sequence, with an AM/PM indication. The Panasonic NV-7000, however, gives you the choice of 24- or 12-hour clock operation, and there is even a brilliance switch to subdue the display if required.

Setting up real (that is, actual) time on video recorder clocks is quite simple (see *Video in the home*) and scarcely varies between machines. The display flashes repeatedly when the machine is first switched on. This warns you that the clock has not been set and stops when you begin to adjust the displayed time. (Any adjustment stops the flashing; the machine obviously cannot tell what the right time should be.) Top machines have a 1-hour battery back-up for the timer to cope with brief disconnections or minor power cuts.

Single event timer

The standard timer – recording one 'event' or programme sequence – is to be found on Hitachi VT-8300, Panasonic

58

NV2000, Ferguson 3V29, JVC HR-7200 and many other budget priced machines. These can all be set to record up to seven or ten days ahead. Below is an early timer display, still found on many machines in the rental market. Later machines use just two buttons: 'select' (to advance between day, channel, time and duration) and 'set' (to execute settings).

Display and controls of a simple single event timer

Early recorders could only be set three days or even just 24 hours ahead – which is how most people use 'single event' timers anyway – but the extra days can be useful to catch a programme during a holiday. Prices vary from around £450 ('basic') to £500 ('mid-range') for the machines mentioned, which are all VHS format. The Betamax format Sanyo VTC-9300 has a timer which can only be set up to 3 days hence (again to record a single event), but this very good value machine costs around £400 (prices include VAT).

Most single event recorders today incorporate a so-called 'everyday' facility. This allows you to record at the same time (on the same channel of course) on consecutive days.

Programmable timer

Since the first generation of home video recorders, a more sophisticated timer has emerged: the 'programmable' type. This allows you to 'programme' the machine with a number of recording events or sequences, from a choice of television channels.

A number of machines now incorporate programmable timers. The most sophisticated of these are the Ferguson 3V23, Panasonic NV-7200, and JVC HR-2700 (all VHS format) allowing up to eight recording events to be made over a fourteen day period. Prices vary from £650 for the Panasonic, which has all the top facilities, to around £700 for the Ferguson/JVC machines (both made by JVC, but with different cosmetics), which incorporate all of this plus wireless remote control (with which you can even enter programme recording event details) and tape pulse indexing (see later).

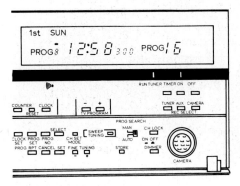

Programme display and controls of the
Ferguson Videostar 3V23 programmable timer

All three machines feature roll-back editing. This is a system where recorded tape signals are aligned with incoming signals (by 'rolling back' a couple of seconds or so before fresh recording begins) to ensure a distortion-free edit point. This is of particular significance to those interested in editing home movies or programme compilations where 'clean' edit points are essential (see *Back-space editing*).

Other VHS programmables include the Hitachi VT-8700 (8 events over 21 days), with freeze frame, frame advance, cue and review and tape pulse indexing; Mitsubishi HS-310 (6 events over 14 days), with slow motion, freeze frame, frame advance, picture search, auto rewind and infra-red control; and the Sharp VC-7700 (7 events over 7 days), with all the trick-play facilities plus tape pulse indexing.

The Betamax format offers the Bush BV-6900 (3 events over 7 days) with trick-play features plus picture search and tape pulse indexing; the Sony C7 with everything from full trick-play (fast, slow, still, etc) and picture search, to tape pulse indexing, auto rewind and infra-red remote control; and the Toshiba V-8700 (3 events over 7 days), with a host of playback features, picture search and pulse indexing. The Sony C7 will also take a stacking device, enabling several tapes to be played

The Sony C7 with Cassette Autochanger AG-9 fitted for automatic tape changing

automatically. 4 hr per side Video 2000 format programmable machines are the Grundig V2×4 Super (4 events over 10 days) with freeze frame, tape pulse indexing, noise reduction on soundtrack and infra-red remote control; and the Philips VR2022 (5 events over 16 days) with noise reduction on sound-track (not Dolby but their own variation), indexing by tape counter readings and some optional features. A cover-branded version of this machine is available from Philips' wholly-owned subsidiary, Pye. A cover-branded version of the Grundig Super is also available from ITT. The top models in Video 2000 have been quoted here; but in fact all machines of this format have programmable timers.

Tape control features

Tape control features include extras such as speed play, cue and review, tape pulse indexing, and the like. They are all refinements in the ability of the recorder to manipulate or control the tape.

To the enthusiast many of these features are useful and satisfying to operate and deserve equal, if not more, scrutiny as the timing capabilities of different models. Some can make life easier for the more casual video operator; while other users may decide these extras add unnecessary complication and cost to their basic requirements.

In any event, it is worth understanding the manufacturers' achievements in tape control before making a decision to buy, so the main tape control features found on today's video recorders are listed below with details of how they work and on which machines they are incorporated.

Still frame

This is the general term for a stationary image created by pausing the tape but keeping the video heads spinning in contact with it. Today's top recorders all have this feature – earlier versions simply blanked the screen in 'pause' mode during playback – but methods of achieving still frame vary between formats. VHS and Video 2000 machines display both

Interference bars on picture when showing a single frame (left); (right) how interference bars can be moved by frame advancing

picture fields in the frame, while Betamax models repeat one field twice to make up the picture. At the time of writing, Betamax still frames tend to be less stable than those of other formats – the picture has a tendency to quiver at the top and bottom – but the post-C7 generation, Sony claims, will incorporate an additional head to improve this. On VHS machines, one of the video heads is slightly wider than the other, to increase stability. Video 2000 recorders incorporate dynamic track following (see *Video Formats*) which practically guarantees correct tracking in still frame and indeed play modes, provided the tape is not excessively stretched (in which case the range of corrective head movement is inadequate).

In still frame mode, the angle of the videotape track is smaller in relation to the head drum because no motion vector is involved. That is why such special techniques, as mentioned above, are necessary.

Slow motion

Permits you to view scenes at a slow – usually variable up to half normal – speed. The angle of the video tracks relative to the spinning heads is different from that in ordinary 'play'. (The same is also true in 'speed play' mode.) Many recorders, therefore, incorporate a separate 'tracking' control for slow motion to minimise the mistracking noise bars on the picture.

Speed play

Usually a twice normal speed facility, operating in play mode only, as with slow motion. Some recorders like the Sony C7 Betamax operate at three times normal play speed in this mode.

Frame advance

Allows you to inch forward a frame at a time with a push button. Keeping the button down slowly advances frames on many machines.

Remote pause

Allows you to pause tape motion while recording or playing back by means of a switch on a length of cable connected to the recorder (normally by a socket in the rear). A golden rule about using pause on a machine, whether by one of these switches or on the recorder direct, is to never leave the machine in pause mode casually – only when you need to. When a machine is in pause mode, the same bit of tape is being scanned by the head drum continuously at a rate of 50 'wipes' a second.

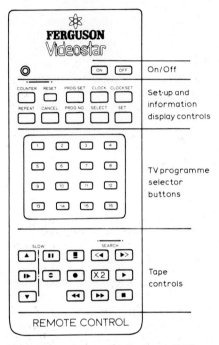

Layout of controls on the Ferguson 3V23
remote control infra-red handset

It is best not to stay in pause mode longer than about three minutes, for the sake of your tape. Pausing for longer than this can cause head wear marks on the tape and ultimately, extra wear to the video heads. Do not 'pause' to answer the telephone or doorbell – you could be away from the machine longer than you expect.

Tape motion remote control

Allows you to operate play, record, rewind, wind, pause and stop modes on a remote handset. This may be either cable connected or linked by an infra-red command system.

64

Full function remote control

Incorporates the above plus remote programming of the timer, and is restricted presently to top Ferguson and JVC models (via infra-red command).

Back-space editing

A technique producing an imperceptible 'cut' from one re-cording to another, and is particularly important in home movie-making. Sometimes called 'roll-back editing', it is res-tricted to Ferguson 3V23, JVC HR-7700, and the Panasonic

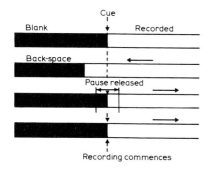

Back-space editing: the recorder tape servo uses time between broken lines to bring recorded sync pulses into step with incoming signals and 'cut' exactly between frames to produce a clean edit

NV-7000 and NV-7200 mains VHS machines at present. Port-ables with this feature include the Akai ActiVideo, Ferguson 3V24, Hitachi VF6500, JVC HR-2200 and Panasonic NV-3000 VHS format recorders. It works by rolling tape back half a second or so from the new recording's cue position, and synchronising off-tape and incoming signals during the run-up to recording. A similar technique is used in all professional – including BBC TV and ITV – videotape editing equipment.

Tape pulse indexing

This relies on a tone being put on the tape at the start of a new recording. During rewind, the tone is detected and the tape stopped. This is a method of finding the start of any number of separate recordings made on a video cassette. Video 2000 achieves a similar result by using tape counter numbers, which you can instruct the machine to find. Sharp's VC-7700 VHS recorder incorporates a pulse-based system called Automatic Programme Locate Device (APLD). This allows you to specify a pulse, x number of pulses away from your position on the tape, which the machine then finds by counting pulses.

Cue and review (or picture search)

A feature which allows you to spool backwards and forwards in play mode at about 9 times normal speed. A similar feature is to be found on some audio cassette decks. It should not be used for winding long lengths of tape, as the heads are closer to the tape than in normal rewind or wind modes.

Auto-rewind

Returns the tape to the beginning or zero-stop point (see below), after recording to the end of the cassette. When you use the machine again the tape is ready to play. Found on Akai VS-5 and VS-10, Ferguson 3V23, JVC HR-7700, Mitsubishi HS-310, and Panasonic NV-7200 VHS, Sony C7 Betamax, and Philips VR2020 Video 2000 format recorders.

Auto-repeat playback

This feature is of dubious value to the consumer, designed primarily for repeated showroom demonstration of a sales information sequence. Unique to Ferguson 3V23, Akai VS-10 and JVC HR-7700 VHS machines.

Zero-stop memory

Most video recorders on the market have this feature incorporated in their design. Charmingly simple, its usefulness is often

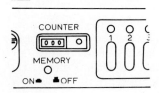

Zero-stop memory counter and controls: when the memory is switched on the tape will always be stopped when the counter reaches zero (in rewind mode)

overlooked by video owners because they have never understood what it is for. A single button normally marked 'memory' sits on the front panel near the 4-digit tape counter. When pressed, it selects 'stop' as soon as the tape counter reaches zero. It works in rewind mode only and is invaluable for a swift return to the beginning of a recording. Just make sure you zero the counter whenever you start videotaping. Particularly useful for absentee recording.

6

Videograms

'Videogram' is a title commonly used to describe a *pre-recorded videotape* or *disc*. Its universal acceptance may be less than certain, but until a better term is found, 'videogram' seems as good a way as any of replacing that clumsy mouthful. An alternative expression is 'video programme', but this can describe a home movie which videogram, by agreement, does not. It is a tricky problem for editors and writers, who rely on words to convey a precise, standard meaning.

Laying aside the question of terminology, what consideration should be given to videograms? Are they worthwhile? Should they influence your choice of equipment?

'Alternative television'

The videograms market is still finding its feet, spurred on by the allegedly mass appeal to which this branch of the industry aspires.

There are many types of videogram currently available and by the time this is published there should be two media: Video tape and video disc (Philips LaserVision and JVC's VHD). RCA has SelectaVision disc in the USA, but no plans are known for a UK version.

Tape is the dominant medium at present, however, with over 4000 titles available in VHS and Betamax formats. Some Philips V2000 tapes can also be obtained, usually at a higher price.

The vast majority of tapes are for rent. Prices begin at around £5 for a minor 90-minute film on Betamax format from 21st Century Video (part of VCL Video), to £7 for a major feature film from CIC, EMI, Guild, Magnetic or Rank (3 day hire).

Many tapes – mostly feature films – may be rented from local shops, specialist video outlets and high street rental chains with an initial deposit. There are also several club schemes. The more expensive rates apply to the major box office successes – *Jaws*, *Grease* and *The Godfather* are examples – many of which are available on rental only.

A still from *Grease* – one of the many feature films available on rental (copyright CIC)

The term 'alternative television' has been coined by programme suppliers because videograms can be played at any time and put the choice of viewing in the hands – or should I say the wallet – of the viewer. This is true up to a point. The consumer can select what he or she wants to see at the most convenient time.

Most videogram catalogues, however, are dominated by the sort of feature films which regularly do the rounds of the television schedules. In the USA this is less significant as programmes are badly butchered by commercial breaks. However, Britain does not suffer that problem to the same

69

extent. Many good films can be seen on either of the non-commercial BBC channels. So a convincing argument against buying many of the titles available is that if you wait a few months you will be able to have it for the cost of a blank tape. As far as seeing, but not keeping, feature films goes, rental offers a solution. By spending around £8, you can see a film in the home about a year before it comes around on the television. For a family, or group of friends, this arrangement compares favourably with the traditional habit of seeing films at the cinema. With cinema seats costing from £1.50 to £3 per head depending on locality, a group of four or five chipping in on a videogram rental works out cheaper than going to a cinema.

On the other hand, cinemas can offer a wide-screen high definition Cinemascope picture, stereo sound with Dolby noise reduction and all the trappings of a night out. Videograms are likely to offer more stereo and Dolby as the necessary hardware becomes widely available.

One company specialising in renting feature films on video uses the slogan 'take-away movies'. It could be that the movie end of the videogram market will see a greater development of the home as a personal auditorium. This would be accelerated by the development of wide-screen projectors and ultimately large flat-screen solid-state home television units.

Repeatability

So far as the outright purchases of videogram feature films goes, the 'alternative television' claim carries a strange paradox. The videogram is an alternative to broadcast television, but both broadcast television and cinema offer a cheaper alternative to the bought videogram.

The decision whether to buy a videogram is dependent on the subject's *repeatability*. How many times would you use the tape or disc? Would you refer to it regularly? Would it soon become dated and boring? The likely answers to these and other questions when applied to a feature film make this a dubious investment unless you are constantly entertaining people.

The best way forward in bought videograms is what analysts describe as *non-linear programming*. This is not as boring as it sounds. For example, if you read *Gone With The Wind*, you would start at the beginning and read it through the middle, to the end. If you went out and bought *Collins English Dictionary* it is very unlikely that you would ever read it straight through. You may never look at the first page and you would not remember 'how it ends' because a dictionary is not read like that. It is *non-linear* reading matter; you read only those parts which interest you, in no particular order.

Broadcast television is quite the opposite. Even fact-giving programmes follow a time-related sequence. They have to begin at an estimated level of ignorance and endeavour to communicate information at a speed and complexity which the average viewer can follow. In practice this makes broadcast television a bad method of teaching. For these and other reasons, most television programmes are not about conveying information. Broadcasters concentrate on the less critical area of entertainment. Videograms are an ideal medium for learning. They not only offer the subject matter consumers want when they want it, but the facility to learn at your own speed, repeat the message at will and refer to specific sections of the programme. The need to 'hold the attention' is removed, because the viewer can simply spool or scan through sections which are of no interest.

These are the programmes with true 'repeatability' and a stronger connection should develop between videograms and bookshops in the future as the market matures.

What is available?

The vast majority of videograms fall into one of seven categories: features (films and TV specials), horror (ditto), music (mostly made-for-video), children's (films, cartoons and TV compilations), sport (filmed or videotaped events and tributes), documentary (filmed or videotaped subject reports, instruction and education series), and what is commonly termed 'adult' (sexual titillation films and made-for-video sequences of varying degrees of explicitness).

Videogram sales and rentals are now dominated by features, with 'adult' subjects, which effectively pioneered the mass videogram market, running close behind.

To draw an analogy with conventional publishing, features are the paperback of video, with other categories taking on the role of the specialist book. The comparison can be extended, with other video media like teletext – the information system carried by TV broadcasts – becoming the newspaper of the TV screen (a function presently fulfilled by television itself).

Videogram producers have their eyes on other areas of paper publishing, too. BBC Enterprises Video Division has assembled a range of programmes it describes as 'videocyclopaedias', clearly designed as reference works competing audiovisually with the traditional encyclopaedia bookset. A videogram dictionary set would not be impossible in this vein. The spelling and definition would appear on the screen, with the correct pronunciation spoken on the soundtrack. Bilingual interpreter versions could be made on a stereo player with definitions given on the screen with corresponding words pronounced on the soundtracks. The best medium for this is likely to be the video disc, with its accurate indexing, fast access, precise still frame, and high information storage capabilities.

Even the high-turnover magazine business could be affected. 'Magazine' videograms could take readers – and more important, advertisers – away from the printed page. The videogram magazine is very much in its infancy at present. Various packages have been devised for the specialised 'adult' audience – from *Mirage* and *Look No Staples* to *Electric Blue* (the latter claiming to be the most successful) – none of which carry any external advertising.

Development of the general, mass-appeal market with commercials has so far been limited. *Rewind*, on tape from Catalyst Productions, is a pot-pourri of animations, anecdotes, humourous sequences and comment, with advertising subsidising its cost down to roughly that of a blank tape. Michael Barratt's Commercial Video has also pioneered the idea of introducing advertisements or sponsorships in its series on gardening, cooking, and DIY.

These are obvious competition to those magazines with similar printed articles, with the bonus that the tape – due to its low cost – can be wiped after a few viewings and used to record something else. Certainly, the publishing industry in general is in for a shake-up in the next few years.

So what is available today? The list is practically endless and would be impractical and tedious to reproduce here. Various guides to video programmes exist, one of the most comprehensive being *Video Index* from Link House Publications. Outstanding items, however, include *Jaws*, *Grease*, *Love Story*,

A few of the wide range of cassettes available from (top) MGM/CBS Home Video and (bottom) from the Rank Video Library

Psycho, and *Barbarella* from CIC Video; *Annie Hall, Carrie, Casablanca,* and *Pink Panther* titles from Intervision; *The Omen, The French Connection,* and *Norma Rae* and *Alien* from 20th Century-Fox Video; *Don't Look Now, Far From The Madding Crowd* and *The Elephant Man* from EMI; *Hamlet* from Rank Video; *Capricorn One* from Precision Video (part of Lord Grade's ACC group), and these are just features.

Documentary material ranges from the story of the Apollo moon mission (Istead Audio Visual), to sex education for teenagers (Mirrorvision) and learning to speak a foreign language (VideoView). Children's videograms are many and varied, some of the best known being *Gulliver's Travels* (VCL), *Black Beauty* (Hokushin), and *Bugs Bunny* (Portland). Music ranges from family favourites such as Abba (from Intervision) and Barbra Streisand (World of Video 2000) to the esoteric diversity of the Boomtown Rats and Average White Band (both from VCL).

Sport is dominated by IPC Video with a *British Open* golf series and *Pele – The story of the World's Greatest Footballer* as examples. London Video – under the name of Video Sport For All – has produced a series of instructional tapes on various sports in association with the Sports Council of Great Britain.

The 'adult' category has yet to gain respectability as a subsection of the videograms empire and almost by definition probably never will. It is largely uncertificated and many of these tapes combine low technical quality with high prices. 'Adult' material varies tremendously from vaguely suggestive old films to sexually explicit made-for-video sequences. Due to the stigma attached to this category it can be difficult to see before you buy and embarrassing to complain. As a general rule, the more pornographic the content, the higher the risk of paying inflated prices.

Videogram producers

Videogram producers, that is the companies creating and/or owning material for video release, are as varied as the titles on the market. Features mostly come from film companies enjoying further returns from old stock, or hoping for renewed interest in their products. Twentieth Century-Fox started the ball rolling almost inadvertently when an American called Andre Blay bought video rights to Fox films and set up Magnetic Video Corporation in the States. Later Fox realised what it was missing and got the rights back – by buying the company. Now Magnetic Video is a wholly-owned videogram arm called 20th Century-Fox Video.

Rank, the multi-national management company with a film background, set up a videograms operation from its existing audiovisual division. Thorn-EMI (now part of the Thorn group), set up its own EMI Videograms company which has since inexplicably been re-named Thorn-EMI Video Programmes and Production. Warner Bros now has its own Warner Home Video division in the USA which is trading through WEA Records in the UK.

Paramount Pictures and Universal Studios trade through a home video offshoot of their cinema distributors, CIC (Cinema International Corporation). Meanwhile United Artists has decided to distribute through Warner and Intervision. ABC has struck up a deal with Guild Home Video for sale and rental. Columbia Home Video is established in the USA and has recently paired up with RCA for distribution. Film giant MCA has a convoluted arrangement with CBS Records to distribute titles on Philips *LaserVision* disc, while that company also distrubutes MGM material through a joint company.

Music on video is slowly attracting record companies, just as more and more publishing houses are exploring video as a medium for their specialised subjects. There are many new-comers, however, with no traditional media background. Video offers tremendous scope – arguably the widest of any medium – of subject matter and presentation style for production companies and people with a wide range of creative interests.

Distribution

The backbone of the videogram industry is made up of entrepreneurial trading companies who have turned their attention – by good judgement or luck – to video distribution. They buy up video rights to features, TV specials, education films etc, duplicate on videotape or disc and distribute direct to users or through retailers or wholesalers.

Between them, wholesalers have developed outlets for videograms through hi-fi, photographic, record, department and TV rental shops. Some can even be found in grocers, tobacconists and sweet shops. In major conurbations like London, stores selling nothing but videograms have become increasingly common. Many of these shops wholesale to other retailers as well.

The main criteria for judging a videogram supplier of any kind are range, quality and price. The quality of tapes (or discs) may be beyond their direct control, but their attitude to customer complaints is not. Your videogram dealer must be prepared to listen when you believe there is something wrong with a purchase and replace it if necessary.

The other option in buying videograms is mail order. Before embarking on this you must be certain that the advertised company – and its range – is genuine. A showroom, credit card facilities and a telephone number are some of the indications of a genuine business; but these offer no guarantees and many highly respectable companies have none. Word of mouth, press reports and professional standard of service are your best points of reference. A British Videogram Association has been formed and this could help maintain certain standards and outlaw sharp practices. As a last resort, most magazine publishers offer a mail order protection scheme, in which your money is refunded if the company involved is bogus or goes bankrupt.

The alternatives to buying outright are period rental and video club membership. Period rental involves paying a deposit of £25 or so, plus a rental fee which depends on the rental period. Rates vary from £5 to £6 for 3 days (CIC, Guild Home Video, Intervision, Rank), to about £8 for 7 days (recent and big name feature films).

The deposit is not refunded if the tape is returned damaged, and it is illegal to make a copy of any videogram. One of the first in the market, 20th Century-Fox Video, did not rent initially for fear of piracy. Confusingly, Walt Disney *only* rents – through Rank – apparently for the same reasons. Most of the major American feature companies are protected by an organisation called the Motion Picture Export Association of America based in London's Wardour Street. This has extensive resources throughout Europe to trace and prosecute cases of piracy. If you are dubious about the legality of a feature, contact Percy Browne (Film Security) at MPEAA (see addresses section).

Video clubs have operated by charging members for circulating tapes between them. A member pays an annual subscription, marks his or her preferences and receives a tape. This tape is exchanged for another when the member tires of it. The clubs also buy in new tapes to feed the system and secondhand tapes from members (or indeed anybody). Video clubs are heavily criticised by the videogram copyright owners as they receive no extra payment each time a tape is recirculated to another member. Under the grossly inadequate legislation currently in force, however, there is little they can do about the situation. Membership entitles you to several exchanges per year, depending on the scheme. The problem with this method from the consumer's point of view is that you do not always get the exact title you request. Much depends on what is available in the constantly rotating stock of tapes.

The video disc

Videograms are not only available on tape, there is now another medium – the video disc. Unfortunately, manufacturers do not seem to have learnt from past mistakes and there are now three separate and incompatible systems, two of which have been developed for definite marketing in Britain, with the third standing in the wings as a possible contender.

The video disc concept is not new. Scots-born John Logie Baird, generally regarded as the father of television, devised an experimental system back in 1928. Contemporary video disc technology is, however, quite different from videotape technology which employs magnetism. The video disc systems of today use either optical (Philips' *LaserVision*) or capacitive (JVC/Thorn-EMI's *VHD/AHD* and RCA's *SelectaVision*) technologies. As they stand at the moment, none offer the recording

Left, the Baird Television Record, played at 78 rpm on an ordinary record player; right, Selfridges were selling this disc in 1935. While the system worked, its quality of reproduction was low and it soon fell into disuse

and erasure capabilities associated with a magnetic medium like tape.

It is this fact which makes the presence of a number of incompatible formats particularly ludicrous. Any play-only medium (like conventional LP records) depends solely on a catalogue of recorded material. Split that catalogue and you create confusion and senseless incompatibility. Fortunately for the record industry, this problem never developed with the mass worldwide sales of single and LP records or pre-recorded

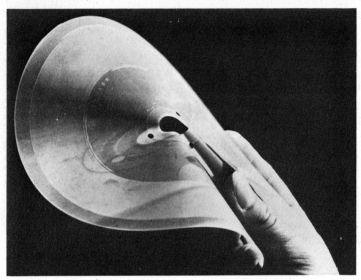

The TeD disc, developed by Telefunken and Decca in 1971, was marketed in 1975, but failed commercially due to the short playing time (about 10 min), imperfect reproduction and a lack of exciting titles. Nevertheless it does represent a milestone in the history of the video disc

cassettes. But witness the fate of *Quadraphonic* investors and buyers. So much confusion and argument developed around the four-channel sound disc that the public gave up. Investors lost money and customers were left with nothing more than a museum piece disc-playing cartridge, redundant electronic equipment and a small pile of discs which would never get any bigger.

There are natural fears that this situation could develop with video discs, or that once having bought the hardware, consumers will be forced to pay high prices for programmes on disc.

Either way, it seems disgraceful that an international disc format could not be agreed; or at least restrict formats to separate television standards territories, e.g. PAL, SECAM and NTSC.

Philips LaserVision

First on the market was Philips optical *LaserVision* system. This uses a double-sided 12 in disc sandwich with reflective coatings in between. Inside each playing surface, a series of pits of variable length and interspace, corresponding to picture and sound information, are coded optically into the plastic in a

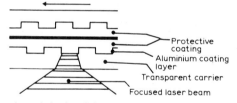

Above left, the Philips LaserVision disc and player; above right, a close-up of the controls; bottom, a section through the disc to show the scanning principle

grooveless spiral. These – together with track guidance information – are scanned by a miniature laser, moving radially across the disc. The laser is driven across from the inside outwards – to accommodate different sized discs – by a servo-controlled motor drive. The reflected laser beam is 'read' by a tiny photocell which provides the basis for television picture and sound signals. Precise tracking and picture sync adjustments are made by mirrors deflecting the beam radially and at a tangent.

Because half the optical information is put on each inner-most face of each disc and the two sides stuck together afterwards, the *LaserVision* disc is uncommonly resistant to handling damage. Indeed, it can be treated more carelessly – greasy fingers, sharp nails, coffee and all – than you could ever treat a conventional LP.

LaserVision players work in two modes: *Active* and *Long Play*. In *Active* mode the disc spins at a Constant Angular Velocity (CAV) of 1500 revolutions per minute and each revolution of the continuous spiral of dots holds precisely one TV frame. This means that still frame and accurate frame indexing

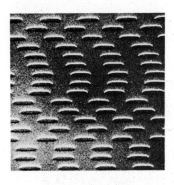

A close-up of the encoded surface of the Philips LaserVision disc

can be achieved by 'parking' the laser on the disc to read a single spiral (i.e. a single frame). Necessary 'wobbling' of the beam to track the spiral is achieved by the radial mirror. By involving the main laser drive, multi-speed slow motion, fast motion, and even backward motion can be achieved. 36 minutes of video plus stereo sound can be stored on *Active* discs, or 54,000 individual still frames.

LaserVision has a lot going for it from the playback point of view. As there is no physical contact with the disc, play life – and more significantly relative to other formats, still frame life – is practically infinite.

Where questions about *LaserVision's* success have been raised is in connection with its *long play* mode. In *long play*, the disc rotates at a speed which varies with the position of the laser, so that the linear velocity of the laser relative to the disc remains constant. For this reason *long play* is sometimes called the Constant Linear Velocity (CLV) mode. It obviously requires a servo control which decreases the speed of the disc-spinning motor as the laser moves outwards. So why bother? The answer is, to increase the packing density of information on the disc.

When you play a conventional LP record, the speed of the stylus decreases as the pickup arm moves towards the centre. The rate at which tape passes across a tape head determines how high a frequency – or how much detail – that system can handle (see *Videotape formats*). It is the same with mechanical (LP records) and indeed optical (*LaserVision*) data streams. On an LP, the level of quality attainable at the beginning of the record is higher than at the centre. Theoretically, a record gets worse from the moment you start to play it. In practice, quality remains at roughly the same (low) level because of the limitations of other links in the recording and disc mastering chain.

A selection of LaserVision Discs from Paramount Home Video in the USA

LaserVision engineers selected a minimum laser-to-disc or linear velocity to achieve the quality they needed and have used the playing time which resulted – namely one hour per side – to create the *long play* mode. The quality from *long play* discs is admirable. The controversy centres around whether such discs can be manufactured with an acceptably low reject rate.

Long play discs carry far more information than their *Active* counterparts. Consequently mastering – and particularly replication – is more critical. Philips is currently mastering in Eindhoven, Holland and replicating in Blackburn, Lancashire and Eindhoven. In each case a process using polymerisation called *2P* is used to make the discs. The video press has been full of stories about difficulties and high rejection rates, alterted by the appalling problems experienced in the USA. North American Philips and its subsidiary DiscoVision have used a different process – relatively conventional injection moulding – which proved to be extraordinarily troublesome.

Since most of Philips' launch catalogue – and a significant slice of its future catalogue and volume sales – will involve features which rely on the *long play* disc, the success of *LaserVision* depends largely on the success of *long play* replication.

In *long play* mode, still frame, frame indexing and all the other 'trick' features are not possible since the number of frames on each revolution varies across the disc. Cruder indexing – elapsed time, for example – is possible. Two players are available: the VP600, and remote-control VP700. Both can play *Active* and *long play* discs. The type is detected automatically when the disc is inserted into the player. This is done normally, as you would insert an LP record but there is no pick-up arm to operate (the laser tracks from underneath), and as a safety feature, a sturdy lid must be closed before the player will operate.

JVC VHD/AHD

JVC's *VHD/AHD* (Video High Density/Audio High Density) video disc system, which has the backing of Thorn-EMI in Britain and Europe, operates on an entirely different principle to *LaserVision*.

VHD/AHD's 10in diameter discs have a spiral of pits, similar to Philips discs. But there the similarity ends. Firstly, the whole system works on capacitance, not light. *VHD/AHD* discs are tracked from the outside inwards by a sapphire shoe resting on about ten of the disc's grooveless tracks at any one time. In the middle of this sapphire is a fine electrode which reads just one track.

Top, two VHD/AHD video players, on the left the Sharp and on the right Panasonic; bottom, the Thorn–EMI/JVC disc player, random access unit and pulse code modulator (for AHD sound reproduction)

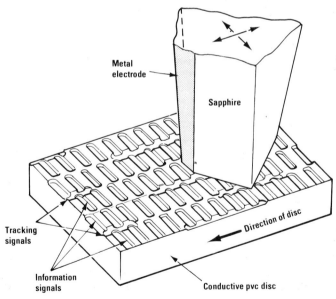

The stylus of JVC VHD system

The disc is charged with a constant voltage through the turntable and the electrode reads tracks by measuring the capacitance of the variable-depth pits in the disc. The disc rotates at a constant angular velocity of 750 rpm; there is no constant linear velocity (see *LaserVision*) variation. The stylus is guided coarsely across the disc radius by a motor drive and small tracking adjustments are made with an electromagnetic cantilever on which the stylus is mounted. Programme indexing is easily achieved, and sections can be 'accessed' very quickly, as with *LaserVision*.

As the disc is spinning at half the speed of a *LaserVision* disc in *Active* mode, one hour of video and stereo sound can be stored on each side; but two TV frames are stored in each revolution. This makes still frame more difficult. (Trick play modes are still possible by skipping half revolutions.) 'Parking' the stylus on the disc under the servo control to read one revolution of the grooveless spiral means that two frames are reproduced, one after the other. In an action sequence, blur would result. JVC claims it will get round this by installing a frame store – an electronic device which can memorise a single TV frame – into players to handle the still frame function. The main query here is how the company will achieve this at a domestic price. Frame stores are notoriously expensive, at least in their current form. Perhaps a cheap single-chip device will be developed by the time *VHD/AHD* is launched sometime in 1983.

The other option is to specially encode discs for still frame and microfiche-style applications by duplicating the same frame on each revolution of the disc. 45 000 frames could be stored in this way.

JVC claims that its *VHD/AHD* disc will survive 2000 hours of playing, which is significantly more than conventional LP records (though infinitely less than *LaserVision* discs) can withstand; but the disc itself is far more fragile. Information pits are not protected by a plastic base like *LaserVision* though JVC claims that disc coating would be feasible. For this reason, discs are to be packed in a permanent dust-tight caddy, which is only removed under automatic loading and unloading by the player.

The *AHD* (Audio High Density) part of the disc's name refers to its use as a medium for digital stereo sound. None of the proposed video disc systems use digital techniques for sound or pictures due to the vast information rate required. By

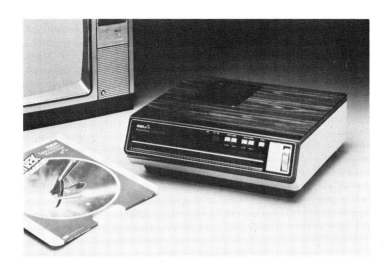

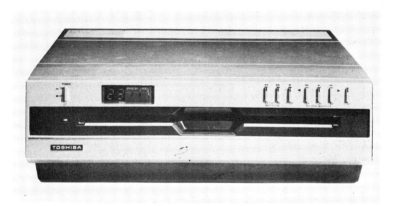

The capacitive system RCA SelectaVision (top) and the Toshiba player (bottom)

scrapping any picture content, that bandwidth becomes available for sound only, in digital form.

JVC players will be equipped with detector electronics so that the same machine will operate in *VHD* (which is actually *digitised* video and stereo sound) or *AHD* (proper digital stereo) modes according to the disc inserted. *AHD* discs – which require a separate PCM (pulse code modulation) decoding amplifier – will not be available immediately with the video disc, but about six months later. Philips has developed a separate player and disc system to reproduce digital sound, which has now achieved almost world wide acceptance as the next audio disc medium.

RCA SelectaVsion

This is the simplest and cheapest system, and the one perhaps the least likely to make it in Britain because of RCA's weak hardware marketing presence here.

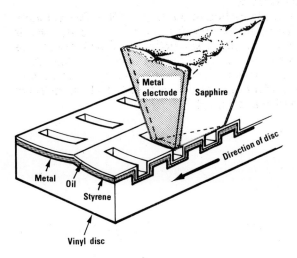

The RCA SelectaVision capacitance sensing
stylus-electrode is guided along shallow grooves and
detects capacitance changes as it passes over the pits in the
disc surface

SelectaVision operates on the capacitive system, but the spiral of information pits reside in a continuous shallow groove. An electrode-faced sapphire stylus with a microscopic curved tip glides along the information pits, guided by the concave groove. The grooves contain just video and sound (which is mono only at present), with no guidance information as this is achieved mechanically.

86

Fast access to a selected section, still frame, and trick play modes are not possible without an auxiliary drive on the pick-up arm which, on the basic prototype, meanders across the disc under its own steam (as with an LP record). Even then some damage to the ribbing between grooves must be expected when the stylus is dragged across the disc (or 'clicked' in the same groove) to achieve these functions.

Basically the *SelectaVision* system is designed to a price, primarily for straight-through playback of feature material. The 12 in disc provides one hour of playback per side, probably running at 500 rpm on PAL versions (that is three TV frames per revolution), and must be stored in a protective caddy. Discs are loaded and unloaded from the caddy automatically as with JVC's *VHD/AHD* system.

SelectaVision was launched in the USA in 1981. PAL versions for Britain and Europe could reach the market by early 1983, if all goes according to plan. Whether RCA, which has the backing of CBS for its system in the USA, will ever launch in Britain is open to question. They may choose to consolidate *SelectaVision's* budget appeal in the sizeable NTSC markets (principally America and Japan).

7

Video home movies

One of the most fascinating qualities of video is the ability to record a moving picture and play it back only a few seconds afterwards. This ability is particularly relevant to the field of home movie-making.

The first time you make a TV recording and play it back will probably create a moment of fascination that lingers for some time until you have grown accustomed to the idea. Your first home movie, however clumsy and unprofessional, will almost certainly never be forgotten. Home movies can record important moments in our lives, family and experiences. Video home movies combine a remarkable freshness with the importance of a medium that is part of our everyday living – television.

Although comparisons are often made between video and film (a financial one appears in *Outdoor recording*), video is really a unique medium. Apart from being instantly playable, video tape is reusable, records a parallel sound track and has a low cost per hour.

There are two ways of making home movie recordings on video. One is to add a camera to your existing video recorder set-up and the other is to use a separate portable battery recorder which is independent of the mains. Adaptors are available for portable recorders to convert them into normal mains machines. If movie-making seriously interests you, consider these combination set-ups carefully before buying any video equipment.

This chapter deals with the first possibility – connecting a camera to the home machine – and also the main points to bear in mind about video cameras in general. Later on in the book the more complicated (but ultimately more fun) possibility is discussed of using a portable recorder and camera – or 'portapack' – with all the techniques and discipline this requires for top results.

Adding a camera

There are two types of video camera output. Most cameras produce direct video and sound signals which must be connected separately to the 'video in' or 'camera' (plus 'audio in') sockets on the machine. Some older cameras (particularly Philips) superimpose these signals onto RF carriers (see *How video works*), which means you have to tune the camera to the recorder as you would any TV broadcast. This method is simple in that a single coaxial (aerial type) connection conveys picture and sound signals together. This marginal convenience is more than outweighed, however, by the degradation caused by the RF decoding in the tuner. For this reason we shall not pursue the RF type of camera further.

The direct video camera escapes decoding degradation by feeding direct video to the machine after the tuner stage. In most cases a switch selects between normal (RF tuner) and camera (direct video) on the front panel of the recorder. A few machines either have contacts on the camera socket which switch over to direct video when a plug is inserted, or circuits to detect signals coming into the camera socket and effect the changeover to direct video.

In any event the video camera connections to be made on the recorder (where no single multi-pin socket is provided) are: 'video in', 'video out' (for cameras with an electronic viewfinder for 'on site' replay, for which see later), 'audio in' (amplified microphone signal from camera), 'audio out' (earphone monitoring of recordings played back on the recorder), and 'remote pause' (goes to the start/stop trigger switch on the camera). This is supplemented by a DC power connection (usually 12 V) to the camera.

For some cameras you need to buy an adaptor socket for the camera plug and make all these connections separately. Others have an optional power unit which incorporates a single socket for the camera and a socket/adaptor lead to the recorder. The third (and most convenient) variation is to be found on top VHS and Beta mains machines: a single multi-pin socket to allow direct and final camera connection; there is no set of adaptor leads or power supply to worry about, as all connections are made on the machine's multi-pin socket.

All portable recorders use a single multi-pin for camera connection. Clearly this is the simplest and surest way to attach

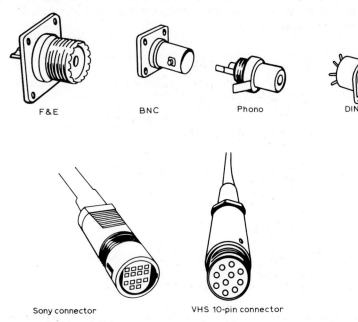

F&E   BNC   Phono   DIN

Sony connector   VHS 10-pin connector

Some of the sockets and connectors used on video equipment

a camera. The age of complete camera compatibility is regrettably not with us yet. Different manufacturers still use different types of multi-pin connectors on their cameras. It is time connections for both portable and mains were standardised, so that any camera can be used with any recorder.

Camera tube types

There are several ways of converting a picture into a stream of electronic signals, which is what any video camera does. One method uses three tubes, where each handles one primary colour (red, green or blue). Another involves just two tubes, where one handles brightness and the other colour. The most popular system uses a single tube with a 'stripe' filter.

The most common today is the ⅔ in tri-electrode single vidicon. Quite a mouthful and still not easy to produce, let alone pronounce. It is a single tube of ⅔ in diameter featuring a stripe filter, target plate, and photo-conductive film sandwich as its active ingredients.

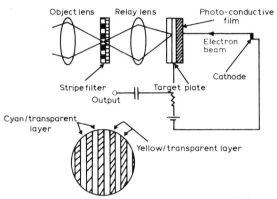

The combination stripe filter detects red and blue (complementary colours to cyan and yellow). Green is derived electronically, to make up the three optical primaries necessary for colour TV reproduction

An optical image is formed on the stripe filters which have colours opposing television's primaries of red, green and blue to sift out those primaries. Meanwhile electrons are scanned across the photo-conductive film on the other side. When the target plate in the middle receives light through the stripe filters, electrons discharge on the plate, which is permanently charged (rather like the anode in valves).

This signal is extracted and amplified to form the basis of the camera output. There is more to it than that of course – sorting out the colours and ensuring that all the lines of picture are in the right position – but this is the principle on which all modern home video cameras operate.

Early home cameras used two 1 in tubes, one for brightness and the other for colour (respectively luminance and chrominance, the two essential ingredients of a colour TV signal). They were easier to produce, but could not compete with the single vidicon's smaller size and lower component count, as technology improved. Three-tube cameras are restricted to professional and broadcasting users, with correspondingly higher price tags.

A recent development to the home user is the Saticon tube. This operates in a similar way to the modern vidicon but has a more sensitive performance. It also suffers less from vidicon's main disadvantage. These are: burn – where a still image is retained on the tube, usually after long *or* high energy exposure; residual image – the tube is sluggish in responding to changes of light and dark; and after image – picture highlights remain on the tube for a few seconds after movement or change of a scene. The last two are particularly marked at low light levels. The life of a vidicon can vary from 3000 to 6000 hours depending on conditions of use, the symptoms of deterioration being reduced sensitivity and focus resolution.

Future pick-up devices

Saticon tubes seem likely to become more common as light pick-ups in home video cameras of the future. At present they are expensive to produce – the JVC S-100 Saticon camera costs over £1400 – but this is bound to change as quantities and technology improve.

The longer term development to watch is the CCD (charge coupled device) camera, currently at prototype stage and a good two years away from production. This is a radically new system of image pick-up using a single solid-state 'chip'. Advantages claimed – and indeed witnessed on the prototype – are improved colour registration, sensitivity and freedom from the image lag problems associated with conventional tubes.

The CCD, together with 'metal' tape, is at the heart of the new camera-corders, of which Sony's Video Movie and Hitachi's Mag-Camera were early examples. Both companies are now signatories to the 8mm Video future standard.

Hitachi has introduced a camera into the NTSC (America and Japan) markets featuring a high sensitivity vidicon tube with a CCD-based 'spectrum sensing system' to continually assess focus resolution and make lens adjustments automatically. This remarkable machine is available in the UK as the VK-C800. As you might expect, a manual override is essential for selective focusing but it is still a very sophisticated development.

The camera lens

As with sti'l or cine photography, the overall quality of the camera depends largely upon the calibre of the lens.

Video camera lenses vary tremendously. The most basic type is permanently attached to the camera body, and has only two controls on the barrel: focus and aperture (which may be automatic, albeit with a manual over-ride). These lenses typi- cally have a limited aperture range (restricting the maximum amount of light that can be fed into the pick-up tubes and hence the overall sensitivity), a pick-up arrangement which suffers from 'lag' effects when a bright light is drawn across the scene and no facility to adjust the magnification to 'zoom' in and out of points of interest in the scene. These lenses and their associated cameras are designed for 'snap shot' taping and are of limited use to the serious enthusiast.

At the other end of the scale – with several stages in between – are wide aperture lenses with adjustable sensitivity, motor zoom and a 'macro' facility for shooting printed matter, cap- tions or photographs at close range. These lenses have a screw

Top, two cameras with zoom lenses, left, the Sony HVC–2000P, right, the Hitachi VK–C500. On the right is a recent Toshiba camera, the IK–1850AF, featuring an auto-focus attachment to its zoom lens

thread (typically 'C-mount') or bayonet fixing to the camera body and so can technically be interchanged with others of a similar mounting. However, the video lens as a separate, interchangeable entity is in its infancy at the present time. There is not a tremendous range over and above the lenses supplied with each camera body and there is much work to be done by manufacturers on standardisation of mountings, colour temperature, auto-iris and motor zoom control voltages and the like.

Many of the better lenses have an attachment fitting to accept a lens hood to prevent glare (on some this is integral), dioptre lenses for close-ups and others to introduce special effects. Mid-priced cameras use filters to change colour and light levels; on top-range cameras both of these can be adjusted electronically on the camera body, or in some cases on a separate control unit.

Zoom

Zoom is an invaluable feature provided (as we shall see later) that you do not over-use it. The zoom control adjusts the image magnification by changing the focal length of the lens, producing an effect not dissimilar to moving towards or away

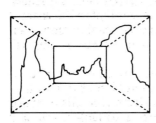 

The zoom control magnifies the image up to 10 times the standard size by a continuously variable zoom lever on the barrel

from your subject, while remaining in focus. It is distinguished on the barrel by a short operating lever attached to its circumference. This makes confusion with focusing or aperture controls less likely and also clearly marks the degree of zoom being used. Zoom is normally specified on lenses as the ratio between maximum and minimum focal lengths – 2:1, 6:1,

10:1 etc, but some manufacturers prefer a multiplication symbol (2×, 6×, 10×). For serious work, a 6:1 zoom is essential. The limitations of anything less will soon become apparent with use.

Power zoom

The top video camera lenses have a reversible electric motor attached to the zoom barrel. These are designed both as a luxury feature and to free the right hand for steering and supporting the camera on a knuckle-grip strap. There are two types of control. Both essentially use rocker switches, but they differ in their operation. The most common type simply selects forward or reverse at a constant speed on a permanently engaged motor.

The S-100 (JVC) uses two stress gauges (electrical resistors whose value varies with applied stress) to measure the pressure in each direction of the rocker switch and vary the motor speed accordingly. Once you get used to it, this system gives the operator more creative scope. The S-100 is also the only home camera to use a *Saticon* (a high sensitivity coating) pick-up tube and is excellent in most areas of performance. This camera also has a manual power zoom selector, which means you can disengage the motor (which simply friction-drives on the zoom barrel). The advantage is that under manual control, the zoom is easily and quickly manipulated. Permanently engaged power zooms tend to be rather sluggish when operated manually.

Motor and electronic add-ons – automated zoom and aperture functions respectively – are very useful but obviously they all take power. This does not matter with attachments to mains powered video recorders, but if you use a portable machine it can run the batteries down very quickly.

Macro

At the 'zoom in' end (maximum magnification) of the zoom controls on some lenses an additional area of movement is provided for certain elements inside the barrel for 'macro' shooting. This is not really intended for normal close-up

95

working, as some mistakenly believe. It is intended for shooting a single-plane object life-size on the pick-up tube, at very close range. Think of how rays cross in a simple lens the diagram should jog your memory). For normal operation, the pick-up tube image is smaller than the subject image. For close-ups, the tube image is bigger. In macro operation, both are exactly the same size, rather like a simplified bow-tie.

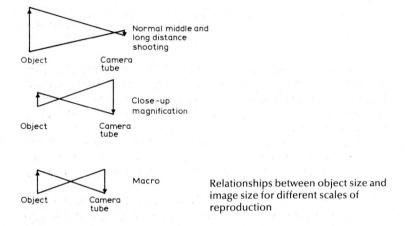

Normal middle and long distance shooting

Object   Camera tube

Close-up magnification

Object   Camera tube

Macro

Object   Camera tube

Relationships between object size and image size for different scales of reproduction

Only single-plane objects – i.e., only two dimensions perpendicular to the lens axis – can be recorded successfully in this way because depth of field at such short distances is extremely shallow. Uses include the insertion of backlit transparencies, photographic prints, or small caption-cum-titles in a home movie or compilation tape. This is a useful facility which is worth bearing in mind when choosing a camera.

Aperture

The aperture control changes the size of an adjustable iris in just the same way as on a still or cine film camera, except that it can also close the hole completely. This position is marked 'C' and occurs at the minimum end of the barrel calibration.

There is no shutter adjustment on a video camera. Frames are generated at a fixed rate of 25 per second. These frames are instigated by a device in the camera called a sync pulse generator. (These pulses normally come from broadcast television when the machine is taping off-air.) However, because there is no shutter, the exposure is controlled solely by the aperture setting, calibrated in f numbers (the focal length divided by the aperture diameter).

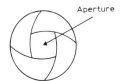

A typical iris in a video camera. The aperture is expressed as an f-number, the focal length divided by the effective iris diameter

On a movie camera, too much light reaching the film overexposes it or (in extreme cases) completely bleaches out the image. However, a video camera uses electronic tubes, not the medium itself, to initially detect the image. Consequently, permanent damage can result from incorrect exposure, rather than just an isolated strip of bleached-out film. This means that aperture control must be set carefully on a video camera, not only for the sake of that 'take', but for the life of the camera tubes as well.

Never point a camera at a very bright object, such as the sun, as this will quickly burn out the tubes. Pick-up tubes are also susceptible to large doses of light energy; a prolonged exposure to even soft lights will burn a permanent image on the tubes. The golden rule is to keep the aperture closed (position 'C' on the barrel) when the camera is not in use, and keep away from very bright lights when it is in use. On the first point, it is advisable to use a lens cap to protect the lens from all light and scratches.

Correct exposure

On all manual lenses, correct exposure is indicated by LED (light emitting diode) indicators in the viewfinder. One is marked −, another + and there is usually a third to signify correct exposure. The aperture barrel is quite simply adjusted according to + or − indications to the 'correct exposure' condition.

Some manufacturers have begun fitting sensitivity switches to camera bodies. These have 'normal' and 'high' positions,

97

sometimes marked in relative levels – like 0db (normal) and +6dB (high) for instance – which control the gain at the camera's video amplifier. So why not use high sensitivity all the time?

One reason of course is that some scenes would be too bright, for example, seaside shots etc. Even in the 'normal' state this can happen, in which case you are either restricted to a tiny arc of the aperture control, or you choose to attach a neutral density filter (which reduces the light by a specified

Correct exposure indicated on a typical LED viewfinder system

factor 1×, 2×, etc) to the front of the lens. Perhaps more important, however, is that picture quality is less in the high sensitivity mode; the image tends to be more 'grainy'. On sensitivity-switchable cameras you should only select 'high' when the ambient light is too low to extinguish your – LED on full aperture. Check that a neutral density filter is not attached before throwing the switch.

Auto-iris

Auto-iris comprises an electronically controlled iris in the lens which plugs into the camera body and adjusts the aperture (f-number) automatically for optimum exposure to the tube or tubes.

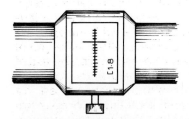

Auto iris meter and manual over-ride control of a typical automatic camera

This facility is incorporated on the more upmarket cameras at the time of writing but will no doubt find its way into the lower priced ranges as interest in video cameras increases.

98

An auto-iris lens can only be used with cameras equipped with a matching control socket but all auto-iris devices can be manually over-ridden. The aperture setting is usually indicated on a calibrated meter which replaces the normal control ring on the barrel. In manual over-ride mode, a small rotary control adjusts the voltage to the iris mechanism direct. On the advanced Sony range of cameras, aperture is indicated symbolically in the viewfinder. Auto-irises work by selecting an average aperture setting for the scene in view. They are, therefore, not very good for silhouette and backlit shots, frequently 'averaging out' the desired effect. Some cameras have a switch designed to compensate for backlighting but it is in these situations that manual over-ride is particularly useful. Note that it is only with electronic viewfinders – which show the actual picture going to the recorder – that you can detect such effects.

The auto-iris automatically calculates an average 'correct' exposure. As the camera travels across scenes with different light levels, the auto-iris swiftly modifies the aperture. This can be a bonus but in some cases you may want dark scenes to remain dark and not be altered to an artifically 'correct' exposure. Once again, careful use of manual control is the answer here.

Like so many connections to and from video equipment, auto-iris plugs, sockets, and voltages are not necessarily compatible between manufacturers. It is best to keep to the same brand as the camera when considering more sophisticated lenses fitted with auto-iris, or indeed power zoom.

Depth of field

This is a more general consideration allied to camera technique. It is the horizontal distance measured along the lens axis between two planes in focus, and varies with the aperture setting. The wider the aperture, the more shallow the depth of field and vice versa. You will certainly have seen creative use of depth of field in still, cine and TV camera work. Used to advantage, it restricts focus definition to the main interest in a picture, reducing background (and sometimes foreground) details to a surprisingly pleasing blur. This has the effect of highlighting the main subject. Depth of field has no natural visual equivalent; but it simulates the focusing of the eye on a particular point in normal stereoscopic vision.

On still cameras, depth of field can be controlled by manipulating the lens aperture and compensating by changing the shutter speed to maintain the overall exposure. Video cameras, however, depend only on aperture to control exposure, but there are some, albeit crude, ways of influencing depth of field. On a very bright day, you would normally expect to use a very small aperture setting (high *f*-number). This would provide considerable depth of field. By using a neutral density filter, however, you can reduce the amount of light entering the camera – without affecting colour. This gives greater aperture flexibility and allows depth of field to be reduced to achieve a greater three dimensional impression.

Some cameras are equipped with a video limiting device – variously called an Automatic Sensitivity Control or Automatic Gain Control – which prevents overloading of the video amplifier by 'limiting' its gain as the output level of the tube increases. This allows you to go beyond the normal setting required for perfect exposure and use the aperture control to reduce depth of field as required. On most video lenses, depth of field is not indicated; but cameras equipped with electronic viewfinders clearly show the effect.

Colour temperature

Practically all the scenes you are likely to shoot are lit with 'white' light – whether from the sun, incandescent (filament) lamps or fluorescent strip lights. Each of these sources, however, gives out a different version of 'white' light. Our eyes and

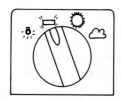

Pre-set colour temperature control. Each symbol corresponds to a known value expressed in kelvins (K)

brain are equipped to compensate and experience a constant sensation. Perfect white light is made up from equal parts of all the colours of the spectrum, but few of the sources we identify as 'white' have equal parts of each colour.

The colour mix depends in broad terms on the temperature of the source producing the light. Actually *colour temperature* is defined as the temperature of a 'perfect black body' (a perfect non-reflecting radiator) heated to producing the coloured light in question. As the colour temperature of a light source increases its colour mix changes, becoming less red/orange, and more blue/white. Sources are calibrated in Kelvins (K); zero Kelvin equals $-273\,°C$. Normal incandescent light has a value of about 2850K, fluorescent about 3200K (an approximation because strip lights produce 'peaks' at certain colours), bright sun 5500–6000K, and cloudy bright sunlight roughly 7000K.

The human eye automatically adjusts to different colour temperatures in the environment. When a scene is recorded through a camera and played back, however, the eye does not make the same colour compensation. The video camera must, therefore, be equipped to do this for us.

The simplest form of colour correction is to use an orange filter. Indoors you shoot normally and outside you fit the filter over the lens.

Clearly this is a crude system and most video cameras today provide an electronic means of adjustment. This is used in conjunction with the white balance control. The simplest of these involves a rotary control with a centre 'neutral' position and decreasing red and blue sensitivity each side (clockwise and anticlockwise). This is really a white balance control (see below) and only approximately copes with colour temperature differences. The better mid-priced cameras provide a three or four position colour temperature switch – resembling an exposure control on a snapshot film camera, though having an entirely different function – with symbols representing bright sun, cloudy sun, indoor light, and so on.

The most sophisticated type of colour temperature control – as found on JVC's S-100 – has a button marked 'auto'. You simply hold up a white card, press 'auto' and electronics within the camera decide what the colour temperature must be for perfect white to be reproduced. A white balance control is clearly not necessary.

White balance

The white balance control is designed to take differences in colour tint into account, though some manufacturers use it as a crude colour temperature control (see above). Colour tints to white light usually only occur outside in sunlight. On a cloudless summer day, for example, diffraction by the atmosphere produces a blue sky, which tints the light. Around sunrise and sunset, the angle of diffraction is more acute and a red tint is introduced. In fact, at the very onset of sunrise and also just before sunset, there is no direct sunlight at all, only diffracted light. It is unlikely that you would want to remove a

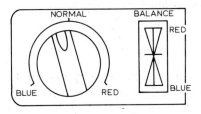

White balance control. A blue or red tint can be introduced to fine-tune true white on location (see text). A meter often displays red or blue emphasis to assist true white being achieved

sunset from the picture, but less extreme amounts of red or blue tints can give an artificial colour cast to a scene. The rotary white balance control, fitted in addition to the colour temperature pre-selector, can be used to reduce camera sensitivity to red or blue either side of a zero position. A white card is placed in front of the lens on location, and the balance control manipulated to yield the best white possible. Good cameras provide a centre-zero meter which indicates colour tint – the centre position is no tint or 'white', and either side shows a red or blue tint respectively. This simple meter system allows white balance to be set up easily wherever you go. Some manufacturers do not include such a meter which means that you can only use the white balance control when a colour TV is available, which is ludicrously restricting.

The viewfinder

The viewfinder is a vital part of the vision recording process, though some manufacturers seem to see it as an area in which they can make compromises and so reduce the price of their cameras. The quality of any equipment, however, depends on the operator's ability to control it and without a good visual (and audio) monitoring system, the movie-maker's control is impaired by having an incomplete picture of what is being recorded. The BBC and other organisations spend thousands of pounds on monitoring systems for sound, vision and video electronics. The monitor amplifiers and loudspeakers used in professional recording studios far exceed the quality of any available domestic audio system.

In the primarily visual medium of movie-making, the same logic must apply to viewfinder quality, albeit on a more domestic scale. The viewfinder must be capable of reproducing everything in the picture and, ideally, *more* than the picture-taking video tube is capable of resolving.

Optical stand-off viewfinders

This is the simplest form of viewfinder which, at its most basic, comprises an eye-piece lens attached to the top of the camera and directed at the subject. Better types indicate frame-in-view boundary markings and indicators for light level (+ and −), 'VTR running', and 'battery low'. There is even a Hitachi model where focus and zoom are indicated by ganging viewfinder optics with the barrel on the picture-taking lens.

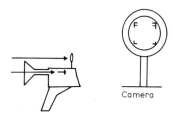

Camera

Simplest optical stand-off type of viewfinder. Note parallax markings on the viewfinder frame grid

Optical stand-off viewfinders, in their varying degrees of sophistication, have one advantage over the through-the-lens alternative, apart from price, they give a bright image. This is because the optics involved are very simple; there is no complicated multi-element lens for the light to negotiate nor additional optics to provide the reflex image.

There is one definite disadvantage, however. It is called 'parallax error' and concerns the difference between the image 'seen' by the viewfinder and lens at close range. As you get close to a subject, the so-called 'angle of parallax' between viewfinder and lens increases. The lens is now looking at an overlapping scene below that of the viewfinder and a shot that appears to fill the viewfinder neatly would, in fact, be chopped short at the top by the lens. A classic parallax-error shot is the talking head seen from the nose downwards.

Most stand-off viewfinders provide some sort of frame marking to indicate 'worst case' parallax – that is at closest range – but it can only be an approximate estimate as parallax error varies with camera-to-subject distance.

Optical through-the-lens viewfinders

The through-the-lens (TTL) optical viewfinders (sometimes called 'reflex'), shows the scene through the actual lens of the camera. It is a good compromise between the stand-off type and the electronic variety. Every change in zoom, focus and aperture of the picture-taking lens is reproduced through such a system, and there are no parallax problems. Apart from eliminating parallax, the TTL technique reduces human error – you can literally see whether the lens cap or filter has been left on, if fingers or straps are obscuring the lens, and so on.

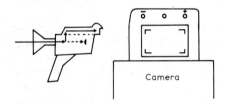

Camera

Through-the-lens or reflex viewfinder with LED exposure indicators above

TTL viewfinders have two advantages over the electronic type. The first is that you see a normal colour image and this can aid clarity for some multi-coloured scenes. At the time of writing all electronic viewfinders are monochrome, even on broadcasting cameras. The other is that TTL viewfinders consume no power and power is very valuable on location work where a battery system is driving equipment.

However, the TTL image can be rather dim under certain conditions and it is only with electronic viewfinding that you can exploit one of video's unique advantages – the ability to playback recordings instantly on location. There are several other features and gadgets unique to the electronic viewfinding system.

Electronic viewfinders

The electronic viewfinder is literally a miniature (1½ in) monochrome TV mounted behind a simple eye-piece lens and (usually) eye-cup. They are found on the more expensive cameras, partly because they increase the production cost of the unit.

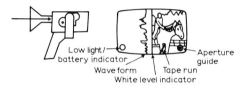

Low light/
battery indicator
Aperture
guide
Wave form
Tape run
White level indicator

Electronic viewfinder. Detail shows indications provided on the Sony model, superimposed on the black and white picture. Electronic viewfinders can show exact camera image or video playback on location

The main advantages are: ability to replay pictures on location (and re-shoot if necessary); actual monitoring of the electronic picture going onto tape (albeit in black and white); and a clear, bright image.

The most sophisticated of these is currently to be found in the top Sony range of cameras. These include white balance, video waveform (showing light distribution in the scene) and aperture indication superimposed on the screen, together with the more conventional light level, VTR running and battery level indicators. Most electronic viewfinders can be positioned according to preference – there is not the essential link with lens optics necessary for optical types – and screen brightness plus contrast can usually also be adjusted. In short, this system gives you the most comprehensive (and comfortable) guidance both to the picture in view and the tape in the making. They are essential for serious movie-making.

Of course electronic viewfinders consume power, but the answer here is to make sure you have a good supply of batteries.

Lighting

The majority of colour cameras on the market today do not accept normal subdued indoor lighting levels, although camera sensitivity is being increased with improved tube and electronics technology all the time. In most cases, however, to shoot after dark requires some additional lighting. A variety of tripod-mounted lights are available, from incandescent tungsten to professional quartz assemblies. For the best colour, all lights being used should have the same colour temperature. Lights are useful if you intend to make a lot of tapes indoors, but you need a balanced array to achieve that professional, shadowless studio look. For this you also need a good deal of space and a suitable background for the shot: a large, light wall area for groups, or a light curtain backcloth for talking heads. Lighting is an art and while scenes can be lit using only two or three lights, a good deal of skill is required to get top results. If this subject interests you, I recommend you study some of the photographic books on the subject – the basic rules remain the same for video.

8

Outdoor recording

Adding a camera to your existing home video recorder can be a very good way of expanding video from a relatively passive entertainment medium to one with considerable creative potential.

There may come a time when being anchored to mains supply – and hence, mainly indoor locations – no longer satisfies your interest in movie-making. You may hanker for the freedom and mobility to make movies as and where you like. The add-on home camera clearly limits the choice of shooting locations but it also restricts the *genre* – that is the type and style of productions – you are able to pursue.

The obvious answer is a battery-powered portable system where tapes can be recorded in a location – or locations – without having to depend on any mains power system. If you are considering buying a video and think that outdoor recording would appeal to you, consider portable recorders first, unless you have an unlimited budget. Portable recorders can also be adapted for use as ordinary mains video recorders.

The outdoor style of video movie-making sounds similar to shooting on cine film, where a certain standard of portability and quality already exists. So how do the two media – video and film – compare?

Video versus film

Video has certain advantages over film. The main one is that tape is reusable and recordings can be replayed *instantly* without special viewing conditions.

There are also certain disadvantages. Picture resolution is restricted both by television's method of picture production by a series of lines (in other words the inherent 625 line structure) and the capabilities of cameras currently on the market. A separate portable recorder is necessary, and is bulky and heavy to carry. Videotape is also more difficult to edit than film. Editing must be done electronically. You cannot splice videotape because the join would damage both tape and equipment.

Even if you could physically splice tape, the result would be very poor because the sync pulses on the tape would be interrupted, resulting in picture roll and distortion. Any television system relies on a regular sequence of lines, fields and frames and if the rhythm suddenly changes, the electronics regulating the process become confused and the picture momentarily breaks up. On video recorders a distracting 'wow' occurs briefly on the soundtrack as the tape control circuitry adjusts.

To avoid these problems a technique is used called 'back-space' editing (or 'roll-back' editing) where the rhythm of new signals is matched to those on tape by a quick comparison before recording begins. The Panasonic NV-3000 and Hitachi VT6500 incorporate this feature. Contemporary models (JVC HR-2200, Sharp VC2300) use fast-start mechanics giving reasonable results. But older portables – and the majority of mains machines – do not and cannot edit cleanly.

Apart from the complexity of editing – which need not matter once you have the right equipment – you clearly need two machines to edit together a series of 'takes'. This aspect of editing video is discussed later.

An important part of this comparison between film and video is of course cost. Super 8 (the more or less standard home movie gauge) costs more than 30 times as much as videotape for the equivalent running time. To this must be added editing wastage. Many home movie makers indulge themselves badly, editing out very little sub-standard shots; sometimes none at all. In fairness they would probably adopt a similar attitude to video movies; but could re-use the tape.

The hardware – that is Super 8 sound camera, projector, screen and editing device (though many dispense with this vital item) could cost anything between £200 and £1000. An average outlay might be about £450.

Videotape costs between £3.90 and £4.50 per hour for those formats in which portable home VTRs are available. Editing wastage is re-useable. The hardware – that is the colour camera and portable VTR – adds up to between £1100 and £1300, making the assumption that you already possess a colour TV. This package does not include 'cutting room' editing like the film set-up. The nearest thing to the relatively simple editing device mentioned for film – which is no more than a hand-cranked device throwing the film's image onto a small optical screen – is another VTR. The break-even point between film and video tape occurs when:

£450 + h × £126 (film) = £1200 + h × £4.20 (video), according to average values and where 'h' is the break-even number of hours, and £126 is the film cost per hour (30× video). So 126 h − 4.2 h = 1200 − 450, or 121.8 h = 750; hence h = 6.15 h.

Although the comparison is not totally complete, an accountant's 'bottom line' conclusion might be that after six hours nine minutes of recording – at which point expenditure in either media would have nudged just over £1224 – the video gear would start to pay for itself rapidly. Of course there's more to it than that, on both sides of the scale. But it may show video to be cheaper for home movie-making than you thought.

The portable recorder

Portable recorders have improved tremendously in quality and particularly in the reduction of their bulk over the last few years, but are currently available in three formats: VHS, Betamax and more recently Technicolor's ¼ in system. All machines operate from 12 V DC power and the old lead-acid battery is being replaced by the more efficient nickel-cadmium type, with savings in size and weight. Tape transport refinements and microelectronics techniques have further assisted this trend towards more compact design.
    What distinguishes a portable machine from its mains counterpart, apart from the obvious difference in power source? There are two blocks of circuitry not included in a portable. One is the RF tuner. You cannot 'tune in' to a TV station on a portable as you would a standard mains machine (though an accessory for this is available). A portable machine records from a direct video source – which needs no tuning in – with separate sound. The other features missing are the clock and

timer assemblies. The basic portable machine cannot be programmed to switch on and off at certain times to record programmes (again, there is an accessory available for this). However, the operation of a portable is very similar to that of a video recorder for the home.

The standard transport keys – record, rewind, wind, stop, play, eject – are the same and most can be plugged directly into a television set for playback as normal. Technicolor has made additional savings on bulk and weight in its compact ¼ in-tape Quarter-Porta 212 by not incorporating an RF decoder in the machine. This device – essential for playback on a conventional TV set – has instead been included in the charger unit (which you would need to buy anyway to keep batteries charged). Doubtless other manufacturers will follow this lead in the battle for low bulk and weight.

Other portable recorder features include an 'audio dub' button for recording sound without affecting the picture (this can be found on many mains machines); a 'dew' or 'wet' indicator to show when the humidity is too high (when there is a danger of tape sticking to the head drum); small heaters fitted to the drum to dispel moisture; 3.5 mm jack auxiliary microphone input (which cancels the camera microphone signal); 3.5 mm jack earphone socket and battery level indicator.

Some more recent models also incorporate 'trick-play' features more usual on mains machines, such as, still frame (Ferguson 3V24, Hitachi VT6500, JVC HR-2200, Panasonic NV-3000 in VHS format, Sony SL-3000 in Betamax, and Technicolor 212 in Quarter-Porta format), (Ferguson, Hitachi, JVC, Panasonic and Technicolor); picture search (Hitachi, JVC, Sharp VC2300, Sony F1); and wire connected remote control of the tape transport (Ferguson, Hitachi, JVC, and Panasonic). Today's portable manufacturers have incorporated tape transport controls of the 'touch-button' electronic type, with LED indicators showing in which mode the machine is operating. The Hitachi 'insert editing' machine (of which see later) even has a cordless remote control. Doubtless this feature will be available in both forward and backward modes soon and will become increasingly common on portable machines.

The most important feature however is 'back-space' editing. This is the technique which ensures that separate 'takes' butt together with no picture disturbance at the join. Only a limited range of so-equipped models exists in the UK at present. Back space editing is essential for compiling a finished home movie (with a sequence of 'takes') on location. Portable recorders cost between £550 and £650 (including battery charger and VAT) depending on features.

The basic portable recorder and camera kit is sometimes called a 'portapack'.

Tuner/timer attachments

The tuner/timer unit adapts a portable machine to receive television broadcasts and switch on and off at preset times, like a mains machine. Most allow only one recording event to be set over ten days (important exceptions are the Hitachi and Panasonic attachments which allow up to eight events to be planned over 21 and 14 days respectively).

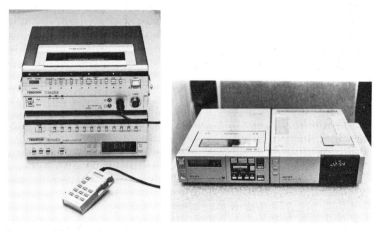

Two portable recorders, shown here with their tuner/timers – the Ferguson Videostar and the Sony F1

Tuner/timers for the earlier portable recorders (Akai VP7100, Ferguson 3V01 and JVC HR-4100) consisted of an RF tuner with channel selector and a clock assembly incorporating on/off timer controls. Modern units provide these essential facilities but also include a battery charger/power supply facility. There is no need to buy a charger separately – everything for mains operation is included in the one unit. In all cases a separate battery charger/power supply only unit is available for those not interested in recording television broadcasts; those fortunate enough to possess a mains machine as well, for instance.

A portable used with a tuner/timer gives normal home video facilities – the ability to 'timeshift', record one programme while watching another and so on – with only one or two of the feature trimmings missing. Those interested in outdoor recording who are contemplating video for the first time would, therefore, do well to consider a portable plus tuner/timer/charger as their first buy. The cost comes to around £800 inclusive (which is rather more than a mains machine) but essentially gives you two types of recorder.

Battery charger and power supply

Whether you decide to invest in a tuner/timer or not, you will certainly need some way of charging the battery after location recording. The simple battery charger/power supply unit provides a 12V DC output plug which connects to the auxiliary power input socket on the portable.

The portable's battery is automatically charged up to strength while the machine is not in use. When the machine is operated, charging stops and the power is used by the recorder direct. Most battery charger/power supply units provide an additional socket for charging a spare battery. A spare battery is extremely useful and recommended for any kind of serious movie-making.

The battery plugs directly into a special compartment in the recorder. It is difficult to overcharge a battery. As soon as the correct voltage is achieved the charge voltage is ignored. Battery level can be checked at any time during charging by disconnecting the charger, switching on the recorder, and reading the battery level indicator.

Charging takes three to four hours for a battery in good condition, but it is a good idea never to fully exhaust a battery. It may never again charge fully.

If you own a car you can use its battery to operate the recorder. The best way to hook this up is via a cigarette lighter socket, using one of the standard connecting leads available from dealers. This method is convenient and ensures that polarity is correct – which is very important.

Battery life between charges

The length of time you can record depends more on the battery than the tape. Whereas most formats can record up to three hours on one cassette, the battery will last for one hour at the most.

Every battery has a certain quantity of power stored electrochemically inside it and it is this quantity which primarily concerns us in assessing its life between charges. The unit expressing electrical quantity is the *ampere-hour* – you may have seen it quoted on car batteries. You can estimate the life of your battery by using this figure.

Firstly, find out the total power consumption in *watts* of the equipment. This is given in the handbook of both the portable recorder and the camera. Then look at the battery (or the portable's handbook) to find out the ampere-hours figure. Multiply the amp-hours by 12 (the battery voltage) and divide by the total number of watts drawn by the equipment, to find the theoretical battery life in hours. The equation is:

$$\text{Battery life in hours} = \frac{\text{Battery amp-hours} \times 12 \text{ (volts)}}{\text{Total power consumption in watts}}$$

In practice, battery life is modified by age, temperature and conditions. Also, logging the time used is difficult on location, because the power consumed depends on how you use the system. Basically this is a difficult thing to predict accurately so it is best to take a spare battery, keep an eye on the portable's battery level indicator and try to develop a practical experience of battery performance. Some batteries peter out slowly, others fall below operating voltage suddenly.

Remember that *any* power-driven accessories reduce battery life, such as an electronic viewfinder, power zoom, tape rewinding, playback on location, tape lace-up and pause mode (the latter is particularly easy to forget). Betamax portables lace-up tape only when a cassette is inserted or removed, but VHS machines go through a lacing cycle every time you go into play or record from stop or winding (and vice versa) and so use up more power. All these things should be borne in mind and those actions minimised if you need to get the most life out of your battery.

Some machines, like the Hitachi, VHS, have a power control so that you can save power in pause between shots.

Recording sound

Practically all home video cameras have a microphone mounted on the body. The signal goes to an amplifier and passes down the multicore to the portable recorder's camera socket. Once inside the machine, the sound is regulated automatically by a piece of circuitry called an automatic gain control (AGC), before being recorded electronically onto a separate track on the top of the videotape. Being separate, the sountrack can be modified by using the 'audio dub' facility but because it is recorded alongside picture information, it always remains in step – or synchronisation – with action.

Video camera microphones are usually of the electret omni-directional (equally sensitive in all directions) type. An exception to this is the microphone used on JVC's S-100 Saticon tube camera. This has a sensitivity pattern – or polar response as it is called – which varies from omni- (circular response) to cardioid- (heart-shaped) to unidirectional (a long 'lobe' of sensitivity in the direction of the subject), according to the position of the zoom control. So as you 'close in' on a subject, the microphone does too – even though it remains fixed to the camera. The average camera, however, is not equipped in this way. There may also be occasions when a separate or more specialised microphone than the camera microphone is required. Several portable recorders provide an auxiliary microphone socket which cuts out the microphone on the camera. Sometimes this socket is on the camera itself.

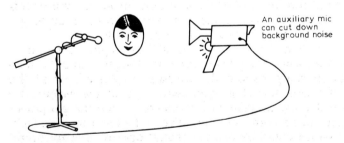

An auxiliary mic can cut down background noise

An auxiliary microphone can cut down background noise

A separate microphone is especially useful for cutting down background noises, which in extreme cases can cause the AGC to 'dip' the sound level and the sound you wanted to record will drop suddenly, creeping up slowly afterwards as the electronic circuitry 'recovers'. An auxiliary microphone directed specifically at the subject prevents this. You can also connect a neck (lavalier) or tie-clip microphone for unobtrusive pick-up. Any standard high impedance microphone is suitable.

A third possibility is to use a mixer. One of the more inexpensive microphone mixers with a 'microphone level' output (such as the 4-way Eagle model) may be used to connect several microphones through the auxiliary microphone socket. These mixers have their own 9V battery power, so there is no drain on the system. Mixing at microphone level tends to introduce electronic noise – in the form of 'hiss' – to the soundtrack. This may not matter as the quality of audio on video recorders is not very high anyway. The best way to do it, however, is at 'line' (amplified) level, using a line level mixer connected to the 'audio in' socket.

Of course, any additions to the self-contained kit of portable recorder and camera make things more cumbersome. This is particularly true with several microphones and a mixer, but even one separate directional microphone takes extra effort. These and other possibilities in recording technique are beyond the scope of this book, but you should be aware of them for future experimentation in video movie-making.

Ready for shooting

The best way to get to know your portable kit is undoubtedly to just go out and shoot with it. You should, however, restrict this unstructured approach to the first few 'trial runs' if the equipment is to become more than an expensive toy.

You should make sure you have all the equipment you need. If you are staying away from home for longer than a day take the battery charger and perhaps a range of plug adaptors if the type of mains socket is unknown. One of the proprietary 'universal' plugs permanently connected to the charger power lead provides a compact alternative. Take any camera attachments which could be useful: neutral density filter for bright sunshine, daylight filter (for older cameras with no colour temperature controls), lens hood (if separate), white balance filter or card for on-site colour alignment (very important), lens cap, carrying case, and – if you have the space – tripod.

Important recorder accessories include: spare battery (fully charged), shoulder-strap carrying case, a spare video cassette, ear or headphones (see *Monitoring recordings*), auxiliary microphone (if applicable) and a pen and notepad. It is extremely wise to always carry a coaxial lead for replay through a television set; you may decide to call in on a friend and want to

Accessories that may be useful, or indeed essential when out on a shooting assignment. (1) Camera with lens cap; (2) portable VTR; (3) filters to match camera; (4) spare battery pack, power supply unit/battery charger and leads; (5) mains extension lead, TV lead and headphones; (6) tripod

show the tape, or if you are staying in temporary accommodation a television may be available for playback. A word with the management may be required in some hotels before disconnected their aerial from the television – it may be connected to an anti-theft alarm system.

The script

Once you have found out exactly how the equipment works, you need to try something specific. I say 'need' because it can take a little effort for some people to take themselves – and their creative attempts – seriously in movie-making. The result of this can be a stream of 'just messing around' video scrapbooks which never find a direction and ultimately condemn equipment to the cupboard.

A shooting script disciplines the user in the same way that a précis helps reporters with a story, or children to write a school essay.

Before you even contemplate a script you need a subject and a theme. The subject can be anything from baby's first steps, or grandad's round of golf, to a holiday experience or a community project. The theme requires intelligent thought. What are you trying to express about your subject? You have the same editorial control which is used to influence the 'slant' or message of news, documentary and current affairs broadcasts. On holiday, for instance, you could present a record of wonderful scenery, a movie of other tourists, the influence of tourism on the community, the night-life, the town waking up, local traders or craftsmen . . . the list is endless.

Most of what you produce will be in the documentary category, so unless you have a story line, your audience will get bored – and you will lose interest yourself. A theme is very important and hence the script which puts it into practice. The amount of detail you want to include depends on your style of working. Two types of script are possible, from one extreme to the other. Find out your preference by experiment but do not be tempted to prune scripts out of laziness. If you ever want to make dramatic productions, you need a detailed script with dialogue and shooting directions.

Monitoring recordings

On electronic viewfinder cameras you can see exactly the image which is going on to tape, albeit in black and white. This type of camera also allows you to monitor recordings as you make them. When you select 'play' on the recorder, the viewfinder immediately switches from camera image to tape, so that you can review your shooting progress as you go. The disadvantage of this – apart from increased camera cost and bulk – is of course an extra drain on the batteries. You have to weigh up the value of a shooting review against reduction in possible shooting time.

Although video recordings always include both pictures and sound, many people do not bother to monitor the soundtrack – they concentrate only on the picture. Sound may seem to be the less important of the two, and indeed there is less you can do to control it, but a defective soundtrack can ruin a recording, unless you plan to dub on a new track (see later).

First, discard the ridiculous earplugs which manufacturers include in their portable kits. These are acoustically inadequate, uncomfortable and have too short and flimsy a lead which tangles easily. You need a pair of lightweight headphones which clip over your head. These are available from better hi-fi stores. They should be of the high impedance type with plenty of connecting lead, wired for mono into a 3.5 mm miniature jack plug (you may have to fit this yourself).

Sound monitoring costs nothing in battery power, and can save a good deal of disappointment from high background noise indoors, wind roar outside, and general noises from clumsy camera operation.

Some tips on camera technique

A creative system like a portable recorder and camera should be used instinctively for best results. If you have to think of the next move to make and how to do it, the effect of the movie will be clumsy. Some general points on technique should be borne in mind, but not regarded as rules to be adhered to rigidly. You must combine or modify any technique with commonsense.

Before you start taping, are you comfortable with the recorder slung on your shoulder? If you are moving around a lot, it may be necessary but normally the camera is better manipulated with the recorder resting on the ground. Some people

A backpack for a portable VTR

use a backpack, a mounting rather like a rucksack frame, strapped around the shoulders. The disadvantage of a backpack is that you have to take it off each time to operate the recorder (with the exception of 'pause' which is actuated remotely on the camera).

Keep all camera movements smooth and positive. The most common movements are pan, zoom, and tilt, in that order. Pan describes movement across the scene in view, and should always be achieved on hand-held cameras by swivelling at the hip. Do not turn from the shoulders or neck – it produces a jerky, less controlled movement and ultimately aching muscles.

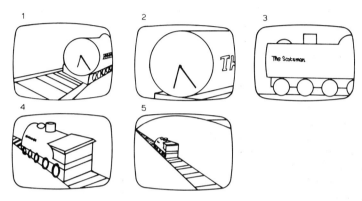

Top row, panning to follow a train; focus must be initially defined on 'zoom in' position. Action is accentuated from a stationary point by a well-rehearsal panning sequence

Pan should not be confused with crab, a sideways movement of the whole camera. Moving sideways, backwards, or forwards requires some skill – you must 'creep' with knees bent – to avoid shake. It is often better to use a different camera angle by pausing the tape and starting another 'take'. Crabbing, walking towards the subject, and going up and down steps are best achieved with special damped mountings, outside the scope of home movie-making. Panning is improved by the use of a fluid-head tripod (see later). Tilt is the vertical equivalent of pan.

Go easy on the zoom

A zoom control is fitted to all good video camera lenses and appears to bring the subject closer to you (or further away) by altering the focal length of the lens. Always adjust focus with

119

the zoom fully 'in' – that is when the subject is at maximum magnification – initially, with 'record' selected but inhibited by 'pause'. Adjust the zoom to the required start position and begin shooting by releasing 'pause'.

Be careful not to over-use the zoom control. It is a typical beginner's mistake, perhaps because it is so easy to operate. Audiences become unsettled and bored by subjects constantly flying to and from the camera. Zoom is a dramatic aid which should be used as such. Mostly it should be used to achieve accurate framing of the subject and good composition. Do not feel you have to use it constantly while shooting.

In-camera editing

To begin with at least, you will be making up tapes as you go along. The method of butting the end of one recording with the beginning of another to compile the final movie is called in-camera editing. You are essentially editing the tape into a sequence using only the camera to select the order of images.

A	B	C	D	E	F

In-camera editing: each take follows the previous one; the order and length of each is decided as you go

In-camera editing is a skilled art at its best and a dull collection of scenes at its worst. As you are relying on one machine, with which further editing is impossible, you must get it right on location. You can replay a scene on the viewfinder and try the following shot several times if need be. Once a scene is 'tucked between' two others, however, the editing decision has been irreversibly made; unless you start from that scene, or 'insert' edit (see again later).

Cine enthusiasts do a lot of in-camera editing, but they can easily snip out superfluous moments afterwards with minimal equipment. The video user would need an additional recorder at the very least to achieve this kind of freedom and it normally causes some quality degradation. [Alternatives to in-camera editing are discussed in Chapter 9.]

120

The right moment to 'cut'

In-camera editing clearly requires absolute precision in defining the moment to 'cut' – that is, halt recording by depressing 'pause' – whereas more sophisticated editing methods need some spare footage at the top and tail of each 'take'.

If you are editing in-camera, how do you decide when to 'cut'? Your general guide here is of course the shooting script but you need to know the effect of different methods to enable you to execute the script.

It is usually best not to cut on a zoom. Wait until the zoom has been completed and a new viewpoint reached before pressing 'pause'. Similarly, if you are moving with the camera, a stationary scene usually makes the best link to the next shot.

Zoom in slowly to start a scene (1, 2, 3); cut to detail (4); zoom into suitable frame for cut (5, 6), pan detail (7); cut to close-up motif (8)

Cutting while panning the camera can work if you are trying to convey action, but only when this is followed directly by another pan, at a similar rate and in the same direction. The general rule is to start and finish each take with a good stationary 'frame' – a balanced scene with correctly proportioned picture components – as though you were taking a still picture with a film camera.

As a guideline, it is best to begin a movie with a general view or views by turning the zoom control to its fully 'out' position. As the production proceeds you can zoom in and perhaps remain so between scenes. Your final scene or scenes should be with zoom out. This is a good rule because the eye/brain analysis of any subject naturally follows that sequence. When you study a painting, landscape or inanimate object, you receive an overall impression first, pick out details afterwards and finish with a general view before turning to something else.

A production technique often used on television is to show glimpses of close-up scenes while the credits roll at the beginning of the programme. This is designed to catch and hold the viewer's interest, rather than an artistic device to enhance the overall effect, and requires complex editing. You can prepare caption boards for on-site recording of title and credits if such a style of presentation appeals to you. Alternatively you can record opening titles before you leave home and tack on the closing credits when you get back.

Use of a tripod

A tripod can give extra stability and smoothness to your movies and is particularly useful when taking long shots with the zoom control.

Tripods of varying height, quality and cost can be obtained from leading video names like Ferguson, JVC and Sony. The camera is simply screwed to the pan and tilt head fixed to the leg junction. Prices start at around £80 for the basic type with barrel-grip locks on the legs. The more expensive ones have proper butterfly locking screws which look less elegant but are much easier and quicker to use. (Tripods designed for the heavier still or cine camera are also suitable, but must be fitted with a suitable pan and tilt head.)

Another feature of the high quality tripod is a *fluid* pan and tilt head. This comprises the usual horizontal (pan) and vertical (tilt) bearings with an operating lever, but each bearing is damped with a viscous fluid, usually oil-based. The advantage is that the fluid absorbs sudden fluctuations of movement. The result is a smooth professional-looking motion as you turn or tilt the camera.
Tripod legs have a tendency to splay out, particularly on uneven surfaces. To overcome this, a flat base (or dolly) is available on some models which has sockets to accept the tripod feet. General stability is improved. Professional bases have lockable swivel castors to transport the tripod in its opened out position. Apart from location work, a tripod is essential for taping captions, close-up or macro shots and 'talking head' commentary or discussion material.

9

Copying and editing recordings

So far we have considered using video with just one recorder, where tapes are put together in their final sequence at the time of recording. Certainly this method has many possibilities in compiling favourite TV programmes and making home movies using the in-camera editing technique, but there are limitations.

Because you can never physically splice videotape as you can cine film or audio tape (due to the risk this puts on the tape and head mechanism), items remain at their original length in their original sequence. There is no scope for manipulation of the programme after recording.

A second recorder solves the problem, by allowing you to copy programmes selectively into any form you choose, the essence of an editing process. A second recorder may seem a rather expensive solution but it is the only way to edit video. Very often the second machine may be borrowed from a friend or an enthusiast's club. It is worth advertising for like-minded video recorder owners to co-operate with equipment and experiences.

Clearly copying and editing are closely related in video, the one being the basic process and the other its intelligent application.

Copying

Videotape copying is achieved by playing back a signal from one machine and recording it on the other, at normal speed. Even professional videotape duplicating companies operate

124

this time-consuming method, using banks of 'slaves' or recording machines working from a master playback machine which
in many cases is of broadcasting quality. In professional audio cassette copying it is possible to
duplicate at high speed – up to 16 times normal play speed –
but this is not practicable with video. The frequencies involved
are already comparatively high and would not be manageable if
speeded up. There is an experimental process developed by
Matsushita Corporation of Japan to magnetically 'print' copies
in contact in a strong magnetic field but this is yet to reach
product stage. All duplicating houses battle on at present with
the 'real-time' master/slaves system.

Many people are confused about the legality of copying.
Basically it is illegal to copy a commercial prerecorded
videotape or disc; you could be prosecuted by the copyright
holder. This is most likely if you were to try and sell the 'pirate'
copy or copies.

As for broadcast programmes, the television companies do
not technically condone video recording of their output at all,
though they turn a blind eye to the private user – indeed there
is nothing they can do so stop it. Some suggest that a levy be
put on blank tape to compensate for alleged loss of earnings
arising from home recording. If copies are sold for gain,
however, they have a legal case against the copyist. Indeed
many cases concerning the piracy of broadcast programmes
have more than one claimant: a film company, music royalty
collection agency and an actors' union may all be involved as
well as the broadcasting company.

It is perfectly legal to copy any home movie material which
does not contain copyright protected visual or sound (i.e.
music) sequences.

Using the 'aerial' socket

This method requires a UHF coaxial lead connecting 'RF out'
on the master machine (the machine used to playback the
original) to the 'aerial in' socket on the slave (or copy-making)
machine. The connectors on the lead will be either coax plug
to coax plug, coax socket to coax plug, depending on whether
the master's 'RF out' termination is male (socket required) or
femal (plug required). 'Aerial in' terminations are always

female to match standard coax plugs on aerial leads. It should not be necessary to make up a lead as the link provided with the master machine for connection to a television will do the job. The slave's link can then be used to 'monitor' the operation on television and check the quality of playback afterwards.

Having connected the two machines, the slave must be tuned into the master's output. Select a channel button not in use on the slave and select 'test pattern' on the back switch of

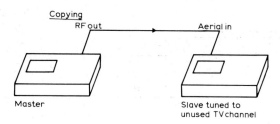

Copying using aerial socket(s)

the master. Alternatively play back a good tape. Following the normal procedure for tuning in a television station, you should be able to locate and fine-tune the signal from the master-recorder into the slave.

When you have tuned in, the picture may suffer from horizontal or herringbone interference bands. This is because the output carriers of the two recorders are 'beating' together. You can solve this by changing the output carrier frequency on one of the machines – scrutinise the handbook and you should find a preset control for this. Be careful not to de-tune into any of the frequencies that the TV stations use, or you will get interference on that channel when you try to record it in the future. You can test for such interference by trying all buttons in 'record' mode on a spare bit of tape.

You can see that this method can lead to certain difficulties. But it also results in very poor quality copies. The original signal off-tape is first encoded with a radio frequency (RF) carrier, then decoded again by the slave's tuner back to 'raw' video. All this degrades quality. It is far better to transfer the raw (or composite as it is called) video signal direct, without encoding or decoding.

Composite video copying

Composite video has all the ingredients of a colour television picture but without an RF carrier component. It also contains no sound, because this is added on a subcarrier in an RF signal. Take away the RF carrier and the sound can no longer easily be combined with picture signals down the same wire. For this reason, composite video copying requires an additional lead for the soundtrack.

Composite
copying

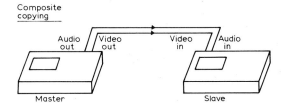

Copying using separated audio and video leads

The video is transferred by simply connecting 'video out' on the master machine to 'video in' on the slave. Terminations vary from 5-pin DIN on the Grundig V2X4 to phono on Akai and Toshiba models. But most are either of the F & E (see p. 90) type (older Ferguson, older JVC, Nordmende, Sanyo and Sharp) or BNC (Ferguson 3V23, JVC HR-7700, Mitsubishi, Panasonic, and Sony).

Your soundtrack lead should be of good quality braided or lapped screened cable. 'Audio out', from the master, goes to 'audio in' on the slave. Terminals vary from 5-pin DIN on Ferguson, Grundig, JVC, Mitsubishi, Nordmende and Sharp models, to phono on Akai, Bush, Hitachi, Panasonic, Sanyo, Sony and Toshiba. Ferguson and JVC use 3.5 mm miniature jack sockets for terminating audio on their portable recorders. Once again, these leads can be made up professionally if you specify the equipment being used.

Whatever the terminals, you must use standard UHF coaxial cable. Some dealers and large video hardware shops supply these leads ready-made to fit any combination of recorders.

There is no channel interference to worry about and the quality of the copy is better. On well-adjusted equipment, up to three or so generations of transfer are possible before serious degradation (such as loss of colour) occurs.

127

Recording levels

The recording levels are again determined by the Automatic Gain Control (AGC). These controls operate separately on video and audio components, so there are no meters to watch or knobs to adjust while copying as there would be with an audio cassette deck.

Copying does reveal alignment error in these devices very effectively. While you may have become accustomed to turning the volume of the television up each time you watch a home-made cassette, a slave recorder expects a normal signal. If this is below par, there is a lot of background noise on the copy which becomes worse with further copy generations. The same applies to the transferred video signal, with chroma-shift (colours offset to the right) and various other defects becoming pronounced.

On the sound side, it is more common for AGCs to be set under, rather than over, the optimum level. Some older machines are adjusted to match older tapes, which cannot handle as high a level as the modern ones. In short, you should ensure that levels are correctly adjusted to standard video and sound levels, for the tapes you are using, to achieve the best copying performance. Your dealer is best qualified to assure you of this or solve any difficulties that may arise.

While copying it is possible to modify the transferred programme, either by mixing in extra material (sound or vision), or by making tonal (bass and treble) corrections to the soundtrack. This mixing aspect really comes under editing, as it is more creative and indeed complicated. This is discussed in more detail later, but tonal corrections can significantly improve copies. To make these you need to pass the soundtrack

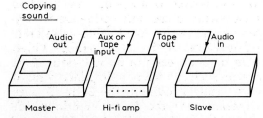

Copying while tonally modifying sound, or replacing with sound from a separate source via a hi-fi amplifier

128

through a good quality audio amplifier, in the same manner as adding new material with the 'audio dub' recorder button. Simply connect the master 'audio out' to one of the 'aux' or 'tape' inputs of your amplifier. Then connect one of the amplifier's recording outputs (or 'to tape' sockets) to the slave's 'audio in' socket. On some amplifiers, tonal control changes can now be introduced by manipulating bass and treble controls and engaging any noise filters, to achieve what seems to be the best sound. You can monitor this by listening on headphones with certain recorders, through the television, or on the hi-fi system itself. If the recorder is too sensitive for the amplifier's output (which is more common than under-sensitivity) you may need to introduce an in-line attenuator (see also *Audio dubbing*).

Assemble editing

There are three types of editing: in-camera, assemble, and insert. In-camera editing consists simply of compiling one 'take' after another into a finished sequence.

Assemble editing involves selecting 'takes' or parts of takes from any number of tapes. These are then compiled on a master tape by using two machines in a copying configuration. Perhaps confusingly, it is the slave machine which produces the final master recording.

Remarkable results can be achieved by this process – especially when post-production audio dubbing is fully utilised – but the drawback is that you cannot pick out a take surrounded by others, you have to start again from that take. So, if the editing near the beginning of a production is unsatisfactory, you have to edit almost the whole movie again to correct it.

At the time of writing, there is no better alternative in home video. You can make inserts (see below), but home video equipment does not allow you to use time-code tape for the precise tape management of professional editing systems. These facilities may be developed in the future. Philips' Video 2000 format has a spare track on each of its four-hour sides which could accommodate such coding, or a simplified form of it. Not all machines are ideal for editing. The Sony C7 uses precise mechanical tolerances in the 'pause' mode which works reasonably well, but the best recorders for editing use a back-space (roll-back technique) at the point of recording, to ensure that no picture break-up occurs.

Tape is rolled back half a second or so from the cue point when 'record' is selected. During the run-up to cue position, off-tape and incoming sync pulses are put in step by the tape transport servo and the new recording made at the blanking interval between the target and preceding frame on cue. This can be found on the Panasonic NV-7000, Panasonic portable, NV-3000, Sony F1, Ferguson 3V23 and JVC HR-7700.

Older machines edit badly because it is a matter of luck whether the new signal is in step with that existing on tape and mechanical tolerances are relatively slack. If you plan to edit with a machine, watch it perform a dozen times or so before committing yourself.

Insert editing

This is only possible at the moment with the Hitachi VT6500 portable recorder. Insert editing is what it says – the ability to insert a 'take' or sequence into an existing programme. This can be very useful in some situations, such as putting together a 'best of' sampler from your library of television recording, or for assemble editing a home movie.

The essential ingredient of an insert editing recorder is dominant recording heads. Conventional recorders use an erase head which clears old recordings from the tape each time you make a new recording. This is positioned a few centimetres from the spinning drum which contains the video recording heads.

Unlike the video heads, the erase head cuts across the tape at a right angle. So when you come out of record – that is, press the stop button – there is a long triangle of erased tape between the last video track recorded and the vertical line where the erase head was switched off. When you replay that section at the end of the attempted insert, you see random tape 'noise' followed by the residual picture building up from top to bottom, as tracks become less and less truncated by the vertical line of erase.

Insert edit machines get round this by driving the tiny record heads on the head drum to overcome the progress of the previous tracks. When you stop recording, the residual picture takes over right at the start of the next frame, because the tape has been re-recorded up to the precise end of that recording, and no more. Erase is disabled.

130

Adding captions

While editing a compilation or production, you may be inclined to add captions or titles, or you may want to do this before you make the movie. There are essentially three methods of producing captions: board, scroll and electronic.

The simplest of these is the caption board, either on an easel or more professionally laid flat with the camera mounted vertically. In either case two reflector lights, each at 45° to the

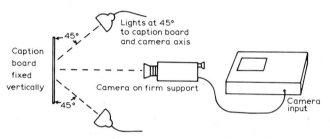

The simplest type of caption is a single card on a fixed board

camera lens axis should be trained on the board. This combination provides reasonable light distribution for a flat surface, does not glare and mostly cancels the shadows otherwise produced on an uneven surface. Some trial and error may be necessary to find the best position. A general rule is to have the lights level with the camera. The main thing is to avoid localised light, or the camera being able to 'see' either of the bulbs reflected – however weakly – in the board artwork.

Stiff artboard makes the best base material. You can write the captions in the medium that suits you best – felt tip, stencil, draughtsman's pen, paint, airbrush – as long as the final image has a matt finish. For really professional results it is best to use dry transfer press-on lettering such as *Letraset*. Draw a thin baseline in pencil on the board and follow the instructions carefully to ensure successful transfer of letters without cracking or distortion. After a little practice, such a system is quite easy to use. Both board and lettering are available from art and technical drawing shops.

A caption scroll consists of a continuous roll of paper or other material conveyed across the frame – usually from top to

131

bottom – onto a hand-wound or motorised take-up roll. Lights are trained on the scroll in a similar way to the caption board system and as the scroll passes across, the camera records the captions as a moving sequence.

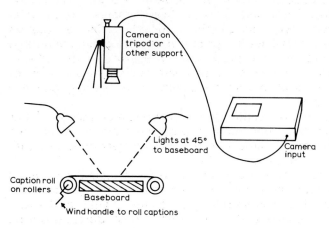

Moving captions can be made fairly simply on a table-top with the camera pointing downwards

Professional units are usually used flat with a vertically mounted camera and are complete with special paper and a direct photo-typesetting system. As is often the case, the amateur has to improvise. Large sheets of paper cut into strips and stuck together form the roll and paper-towel roll dispensers can be used to convey this across a flat surface board. By spending a bit more money, you can buy a hand-cranking device of the type used for overhead projectors at modest cost from a good art or photographic shop.

The simplest way of achieving a scroll effect is to draw the captioned paper strip in a straight line slowly across the camera's field of view. You must be sure that the paper remains flat in the picture and avoid jerky motion.

Electronic captioning normally requires an electronic character generator, which is extremely expensive. However the Philips G7000 programmable television game system has a cartridge called Cryptogram where you are supposed to guess a short sentence 'hidden' in the electronics by your opponent. An additional cartridge allows you to 'scroll' sentences from right to left at a predetermined rate. By plugging this unit into a video recorder instead of the television set, captions can be generated, in colour. So if you like television games as well, the G7000 is good value for electronic captioning. A camera is not required, of course.

Most broadcast captions are made from artwork on a scroll or boards. Black and white vertical cameras are used, in conjunction with an electronic device called a 'caption colouriser' on which the producer can select any colours to correspond with the black and white parts of the artwork respectively. In the case of the board method, two assemblies are often used to provide continuity by mixing between caption cameras.

To superimpose captions over pictures, two video machines are necessary – one for playback, the other to record the captioned master tape – unless you are recording live with more than one camera.

The best captions are simple ones of high legibility and good contrast, with the number of colours and typefaces kept to a minimum. They should reflect the content matter of the tape and not overshadow it. The correct display duration can be found by experiment, but it is usually 2–5 sec for each individual caption frame. Titles (including 'The End') should stay on a little longer.

Vision mixing

To combine video playback with a caption camera signal, you need a vision mixer. In professional circles these cost a lot of money and have many complex features. Sony has produced, however, an extremely useful unit which can mix two sources – black and white or colour – together into one video output. Panasonic has a version with a black and white camera.

The video output goes to the 'video in' socket of the recorder. The inputs could be either video playback machines or video cameras; both operate at the same level. The most common combination is a playback machine on the colour input and a caption camera on the black and white input. This input, like any monochrome circuit, accepts a colour signal. It simply ignores the colour content. (Similarly any colour circuit accepts a monochrome source, though this of course does not transform it into colour!) The black and white input on the Sony is equipped with colouriser controls. This means that the

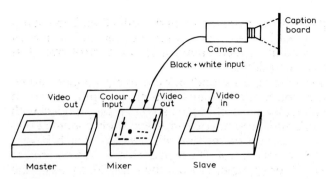

Camera

Caption board

Black + white input

Video out

Colour input

Video out

Video in

Master

Mixer

Slave

Adding captions (static or moving) to a tape to produce the final master tape

captions – and their backgrounds – can be coloured as required. Vision faders allow the captions to be introduced smoothly and master fades can be made to black between sections or at the end of the production. Certainly a very handy unit for the serious enthusiast and it is moderately priced.

Audio dubbing

This is not something to put on your football boots but a facility to record the soundtrack only, without affecting the picture. It is achieved by using a split erase head which can be switched to erase the tape soundtrack only and by keeping the video heads in playback mode during 'audio dub'. At its crudest, the 'audio dub' button can be used with a microphone to commentate on some recorded action but not all mains recorders have a microphone socket, perhaps because such voice tracks are rarely very satisfactory.

If you have been shooting on location, however, you may have caught wind noise on the microphone and need to replace the soundtrack with an unimpaired recording of ambient noise. By using the camera's inbuilt microphone only and the 'audio dub' button on the portable, this can be done very well. Finishing off productions in the home (or studio as it is fast becoming!), can demand more options than a simple microphone can provide. You may, for instance, want to bring an in-camera edited location tape together by adding music, effects, and perhaps commentary, or introduce relevant effects

134

and link pieces to an assemble-edited production. The sound-track has a great influence on a visual sequence. Fortunately video is a medium which allows a lot of control over this without too much difficulty.

To optimise the tape's soundtrack creatively, connect 'audio in' to one of the hi-fi amplifier's recording output sockets. If you have difficulty in matching the amplifier output level with the recorder's audio input, you can alternatively connect up to a tape deck (cassette or reel-to-reel), most of which have a master output level control. The tape deck can then be used to feed sound either off-tape, or from the amplifier by using the recording input controls in a straight-through arrangement. You may have to engage 'record' to achieve this.

Where a tape deck is being used to control the sound in this way, set the level by listening on the television until increasing the output fader on the deck no longer affects the television volume. You have now reached saturation point on the video recorder's AGC (Automatic Gain Control). Take the tape level down a little – to prevent the possibility of distortion. The level you have now defined should be comparable to the volume of normal television recordings made on the video machine. Mark the position of the tape deck output control for easy reference with a Chinagraph or similar wax pencil.

The advantage of using a tape deck for audio dubbing is that its recording input controls keep the level of the sources passing through the hi-fi amplifier on a par with sound coming off the audio tape.

Adding sound effects

Videotape recorders commonly have only one soundtrack. So you do not add sounds by using 'audio dub' you merely replace the existing soundtrack with a new one. This can be fine for linking sections by music. You can afford to lose the original sound snippets from the assembled 'takes' and replace them with a thematic piece of music which unifies the whole sequence.

There may be times, however, when you want sounds from the action as a background noise, to reduce the detachment of a commentary or music. This is particularly true with sound effects, of course, which can sound ridiculous in isolation but convincing in context. The answer is to dub the original soundtrack from the video sequences onto a tape deck, mix in the extra ingredients and record it back onto the videotape. This is called post-production sound mixing, and is an area with many exciting possibilities. With high quality video equipment, the results can look extremely professional.

To dub the video soundtrack onto tape is easy. Simply connect 'audio out' to the 'aux' or 'tuner' input of your hi-fi amplifier, as you would when simply listening through the system. The tape deck is fed the signal when the input is selected. You now adjust the recording level on the deck appropriately and dub the soundtrack.

The next stage – adding the effects, music, or commentary – requires a sound mixing capability. Most cassette decks do not have this, but some reel-to-reel recorders have a 'sound-on-sound' feature which allows you to 'bounce' sound from one pre-recorded track to the other, adding extra material in the process.

On a reel-to-reel deck, and some better quality cassette decks, you have another option. You can record the soundtrack on one tape track, and devote the other to sound effects etc. When it comes to transferring both back onto the videotape, you manipulate each output fader to achieve the right balance. Both output channels of the deck must obviously be joined together in the lead connecting it to the video recorder's 'audio in' socket. Alternatively, you may be able to select mono on the hi-fi amplifier, if you are using this to feed the recorder.

Keeping post-production sound in synchronisation with the video action is the most difficult thing to achieve in home video sound mixing. You must log a 'clapperboard' position where a certain distinctive sound matches a precise point in the action and use this throughout the process as a guide or 'sync' mark. Even then, error through tape slip is bound to occur. This method is not recommended where lip synchronisation – which is very critical – is required. You should nevertheless experiment with this and find out your own and your equipment's limitations.

A final word on audio dubbing. What you see on the screen while dubbing direct remains in sync with the replacement soundtrack. When you play the finished tape back, the sound is in the same position relative to the action. Slip can only occur when post-production mixing is involved. Even this problem will be resolved when twin-soundtrack recorders become common for stereo and bilingual video programmes and ultimately stereo television broadcasts.

The soundtrack is the final touch to a video production and has an important bearing on the overall effect. While a picture may be worth a thousand words, a well-scripted commentary with convincing ambient sounds and some carefully selected music lends shape and direction to the picture sequence. Whether you decide to use some of the sophisticated techniques detailed above or not, the best result will be achieved when the soundtrack is given due consideration before shooting or editing. This is a further reason for proper planning of the script and the combination should result in an effective, smooth-flowing production.

Exchanging videotapes

Television throughout the world has a vast range of different standards. This makes worldwide television reception extremely difficult on one set. You need a vast number of switches to accommodate all the variations which, for one reason or another, distinguish the broadcasts from the various countries. So what are these differences and how do these affect the exchange of tapes with relatives and friends abroad?

Basically, there are three systems of colour television picture production: PAL (Phase Alternate Line) in Britain, Australia, and most of Europe; NTSC (National Television Standards Committee), the pioneering system on which PAL was based, in America, Canada and Japan; and SECAM (meaning Sequential Colour with Memory) in France and the USSR.

The complication arises in the variations to these basic systems adopted for the *broadcasting* of television throughout the world. Britain and Northern Ireland for instance are unique in using a 6MHz sound carrier spacing (at the insistence of the BBC). All other PAL countries use 5.5MHz. This means that you cannot tune to picture and sound simultaneously in other PAL countries on a TV set designed for Britain. There are further differences in the way picture information is coded between countries in the same system group.

All this is defined by the *television standard* in use by specific countries. The technical distinctions are rather academic but the rule is that to receive or record television in a specific country you must have a television set or video recorder conforming to that standard, as well as being in the same system group (PAL, NTSC or SECAM).

Fortunately, videotape exchanging is less complicated. When you make a recording, the broadcasting method nuances are thankfully lost, as the machine's tuner decodes the signal into a recordable form. So the only consideration – with the exception of Brazil, which uses a strange PAL variation with only 525 lines – is the *system* group. Exchange to or from any country in the same system group – in Britain's case, PAL – is fine, as long as the tape format is the same. The chart shows the countries with which you can exchange in the PAL system group without difficulty.

PAL system countries compatible with UK for videotape exchange

Country	Standard	Country	Standard
Afghanistan	D	Libya	B
Algeria	B	Luxembourg	C
Argentina	N	Malaysia	B
Australia	B	Netherlands	BG
Austria	BG	New Zealand	B
Bahrain	B	Nigeria	B
Bangladesh	B	Norway	B
Belgium	BG	Oman	BG
Brunei	B	Pakistan	B
Canary Islands	B	Portugal	BG
China	D	Qatar	B
Denmark	B	Sierra Leone	B
Eire	I	Singapore	B
Finland	BG	South Africa	I
West Germany	BG	Spain	BG
Ghana	B	Sudan	B
Gibraltar	B	Sweden	BG
Greece	B	Switzerland	BG
Hong Kong	I	Tanzania	B
Iceland	B	Thailand	BM
Indonesia	B	Turkey	B
Italy	BG	Uganda	B
Jordan	B	United Arab Emirates	B
Kenya	B	United Kingdom	I
Kuwait	B	Yugoslavia	BH
Libera	B	Zambia	B

10

Video care

Video recorders are complex pieces of electromechanical hardware with a large number of components which could go wrong. Despite this they are remarkably reliable, with faults generally occurring on the mechanical components. Much of this relates to wear (which is to be expected) or misalignment (which must be corrected). Actual premature failure is extremely uncommon.

Looking after a video recorder and its tapes is largely a matter of common sense. The equipment is designed for easy operation and incorporates a number of safeguards. There are no tools required and all servicing should be carried out by a qualified dealer or engineer. (The qualification should relate specifically to your machine type and model.)

Modern electronic components scarcely suffer any appreciable wear at all. The main service routine, recommended every year, is a thorough cleaning of the tape path and inspection for mechanical wear. This includes cleaning of the tape heads, and if necessary, their replacement. If you own a machine, you may be interested in taking out a service contract which includes this inspection after the machine's initial warranty has expired. Some schemes incorporate a head replacement, while others guarantee a replacement machine should major servicing be required for your own model. You can enquire about these options from your dealer.

However most of the initial – and some of the later – difficulties which users experience are caused by operator error or ignorance. Some typical complaints and their solutions, together with general tips on how to get the best from your video equipment, are listed below.

1. Fuzzy picture and distorted sound

Check the tuning on the VTR channel selector concerned. If it is bad on a trusted recording as well, check tuning on the television.

2. Black and white picture

Make sure the broadcast was in colour, if it was, check the switch at the back labelled CH. SET/MONO/COLOUR/AUTO or similar. It should be set to AUTO. The COLOUR position can be used, but when a black and white transmission comes up the machine tries to find colour and an unwanted hue may appear on the picture.

3. Picture colour shifts from the image on playback

This is caused by chroma delay. The machine needs attention.

4. Diagonal colour lines covering the picture

This usually happens when you first start using a cold machine. It is a mild head mistracking and should clear after about ten minutes.

5. 'Herringbone' interference on the screen

Probably caused by the VTR being too near the television, or the recorder's RF output channel may be too close to a broadcast channel. This can be adjusted on a preset in the base or rear panel, but if in doubt consult your dealer.

6. Borrowed tapes give bad colour and confusion at the bottom

The VTR heads are mistracking badly. Try the tracking control. If this does not improve it, try a trusted pre-recorded tape. If the same result occurs, either the head drum speed or tape speed needs adjusting. If the pre-recorded tape plays satisfactorily, the recorder the borrowed tape was made on needs adjusting.

7. Short fine white lines darting across the screen

Tape dropout, which occurs when the tape has shed its oxide in places. It could be that the video heads stick out too far and are consequently damaging the tape or clogging prematurely.

8. Diagonal white stripe appearing on some parts of the tape

This is caused by a crease in the tape parallel to its edges. A less likely cause is a band of grease. If it is only the sound that is bad or the picture slips, the tape is similarly fouled at the edges. All-over creasing can occur due to a cassette manufacturing problem or in some cases, by heads overheating after protracted use and damaging the tape. (This is rare except in arduous industrial situations.) A similar effect can occur if a VTR is left on pause for a long time, although a more common indication of this would be oxide removal at that point, causing white lines of dropout on playback.

9. The picture goes grainy on playback

The video heads have become clogged with stray oxide from the tape. It could be that a particular tape sheds a lot of oxide. The helical scanning is essentially a self-cleaning process, provided the level of shedding is not too high. Try playing another tape to clear it. If this does not work it is time to have the video heads cleaned. Ask your dealer to do this – he is then responsible if he damages the heads, which is easy to do! Ask him to check the protrusion of the heads from the head drum. They may be set proud of the drum surface and consequently may be causing too much friction. If the picture is still grainy, the heads may be worn out. The dealer can check this while cleaning and fit new heads if necessary.

Video do's and don'ts

Some general rules to remember about home video are listed below. Most are a matter of commonsense but you may notice something which does not correspond with your present system of operation or storage. By following these guidelines you can minimise the likelihood of failure or damage, while prolonging the life of your system and the enjoyment it gives you and your family.

The recorder

1. Ensure that the correct fuse (3 A) is fitted to the mains plug and that the equipment is properly earthed at the plug where applicable.
2. Never attempt to operate a machine when it has just been brought in from the cold. Give it time to acclimatise to warm surroundings.
3. Protect the recorder from vibration or shock, or very humid or dusty environments. For this last reason, do not stand a recorder directly on carpet. As the machine warms up, the small dust particles nestling in any carpet are sucked into the machine and this may affect performance and component life.
4. Invest in a good service every year. This includes head replacement if necessary, a thorough clean and a check on mechanical wear and electronic alignment. If heads are not replaced, ask the dealer to assess life remaining and have the heads replaced after that time.
5. Ensure that the video cassette you purchase is of the same format as your machine.
6. Never tamper with a machine – call a qualified engineer if you encounter any problems.
7. Never attempt to splice videotapes. The join can damage your machine which in turn can damage or destroy the tape.

Video cassettes

1. Never touch the oxide side of a video cassette – finger grease and moisture affect the performance and may jeopardise the delicate video heads.
2. Store cassettes in an even, moderate temperature in a dust free atmosphere. Avoid very humid environments – for instance, near a kitchen or bathroom.
3. Always replace cassettes in the sleeve provided when not in use, with the tape edge farthest from the sleeve's opening.

142

4. When operating spooling modes on the recorder (i.e. fast forward or rewind) avoid throwing loops of tape when selecting stop. This is easily done by operating each button positively one at a time. Tapes can sometimes be creased as the loop slack is taken up – although video recorders cope with this much better as a rule than most audio cassette decks.
5. Tapes should be stored vertically, not horizontally or leaning at an angle. Vertical storage preserves the shape of the tape 'pancake' and so minimises the danger of warping.
6. Never put cassettes on a warm surface like a television or other electrical equipment. Warping could result. Similarly keep them away from heaters.
7. Keep tapes away from magnetic sources. Partial or complete erasure can result. Typical things to avoid are loudspeakers, transformers (built into most electronic mains equipment), microphones, headphones and of course TV sets, particularly colour sets.

11

Glossary

Acceptance angle   Horizontal width of vision of camera.
Amp (A)   Unit of electrical current flow.
Amplitude modulation (AM)   Variation in intensity of a nominally fixed-frequency carrier.
Aspect ratio   Ratio between height and width of a picture (3:4 in television).
Attenuator   Device designed to reduce the strength of an optical, acoustic or electronic signal.
Audio dub   Facility on VTR permitting separate recording of soundtrack only.
Automatic Gain Control (AGC)   Device reducing the dynamic range of an electronic signal.
Azimuth   Angle between a magnetic tape head gap and the plane of head-to-tape motion.
Backlight   Light aimed from behind a subject towards a camera, emphasising subject outline.
Back-space editing   Editing feature on a VTR where tape is wound back a few seconds after each 'take'. New recording (the fresh take) is then inhibited until off-tape and incoming sync signals are in step. Result is roll-free (no picture disturbance) edit between takes. Feature of latest Panasonic and Sony machines.
Bearding   Overflow of black into adjacent white areas, generally caused by overloading.
Betamax   ½in video cassette format developed by Sony (Japan).
Bi-directional microphone   Microphone with normally equal sensitivity to sound arriving from front or rear.

144

Black level clamp   Holds the black level of a TV picture at a fixed brightness. Low cost monochrome sets often omit this and black level varies with brightness.

Boom   Microphone or lighting support set nominally parallel with the floor. Usually held by a vertical stand.

BREMA   British Radio and Electrical Manufacturers Association.

Bulk eraser   Device designed for fast erasure of magnetic recordings.

Capstan   Primary source of tape drive motion in a magnetic recorder.

Cartridge   An enclosed recording medium comprising a single reel of tape or film within a nominally dustproof container.

Cassette   An enclosed recording medium comprising supply and take-up reels of tape or film within a nominally dustproof container.

Ceefax   BBC trade name for its television linked teletext system.

Chromakey   Technique which allows a vision mixer to substitute a saturated colour (usually blue or yellow) in a picture for another source (captions, slides, film).

Chrome dioxide tape   Recording tape with higher coercivity and remanence than ferric oxide tape.

Chrominance   Colour component of a television picture.

Coincident Microphones   Two directional microphones spaced at the same distance apart as human ears and angled approximately 90° to each other (45° to soundstage centre).

Colour separation overlay (CSO)   see *Chromakey*.

Compander   Combined compressor and expander.

Complimiter   Combined compressor and limiter.

Compressor   Device restricting the dynamic range of a signal to a pre-determined narrower range.

Contact microphone   Microphone designed to detect sound vibrations transmitted through a solid.

Control track   Track on video carrying longitudinal speed control pulses, recorded and read by a single fixed head.

Crab   Shifting of a camera or microphone sideways. Not to be confused with *Pan*.

Crash editing   Switching a magnetic recorder direct from playback into record.

Credits   Programme opening or end titles.

Cross fade   Slow mix between two audio or video signal sources during which both sources temporarily overlap.

CRT Cathode ray tube. Display on TV receivers and monitors.

Cue track Secondary track on Video 2000 format available for electronic labelling or additional audio.

Decibel (dB) Logarithmic measure of relative intensity, power or voltage.

Dissolve See *Cross fade*.

Dolly Sliding or pivoted member for moving a camera to or from its subject.

Dropout Momentary flaw in the signal-sensitive surface of a recording medium.

Dropout compensator Device which reduces subjective effect of dropout on a reproduced video tape, by repeating a previous (stored) line.

Drum Rotating component containing video heads in a helical scan VTR.

Dynamic range Variation between the strongest signal capable of being handled by a device and the inherent noise level.

Editing Assembling a programme by transposing or combining separately recorded sequences.

E-60, E-120, E-180, E240 Designations for VHS video cassettes of one, two, three and four hours running length.

Fader Creative amplitude control on a sound or vision mixer.

Field Even or odd line component of a frame in interlaced television containing 312½ lines in Europe.

Flutter Variation in speed of a recording medium, occurring in excess of 15 times per second.

Flying erase Facility for erasing single video tracks from a rotating head instead of a fixed erase head. Not found on domestic machines (yet).

F number Camera iris calibration obtained through dividing the focal length by the effective iris diameter.

Frame Stationary television or film image. In European television, 25 frames are displayed each second to give an illusion of continuous movement. Each frame holds 625 lines, composed of two interlocking *fields*.

Frame store Digital device electronically storing two fields, or one TV frame.

Frequency modulation (FM) Variation in frequency of a nominally fixed-intensity carrier.

Gain Ratio of amplification expressed in decibels.

Guide In a magnetic recorder, an indented pillar employed to stabilise angle of tape passing through a tape transport.

Helical scan Method of video tape scanning in which the tape forms a helix round a rotating drum containing two video heads.

Hertz (Hz) Unit of frequency; one cycle per second equals one Hertz.

High energy tape Tape with higher coercivity/retentivity than ferric oxide. Typically chrome dioxide or cobalt-doped ferric oxide.

IBA Independent Broadcasting Authority. Licenses ITV and independent local radio stations and transmits their programmes.

Impedance Electrical resistance to alternating current.

Index counter Device counting revolutions of take-up video cassette spool to provide simple indexing. Relationship between this reading and time elapsed is not linear. Most entirely mechanical; a few use timer LED array for readout.

Inter-carrier spacing Bandwidth separating video and audio signal carriers in TV broadcasts. Discrepancy exists on the figure between UK and European PAL standards (5.5MHz and 6MHz respectively), making simultaneous reception of sound and picture in the UK impossible on European equipment, and *vice versa*.

Iris Ajustable orifice for reducing light intensity in a TV camera.

Kilo (k) 1000.

Lavalier Microphone suspended from a commentator's neck.

LED Light Emitting Diode.

Luminance Brightness component of a video signal.

Lux Unit of illumination.

L-250, L-500, L-750, L-830 Designations for Betamax video cassettes of one, two, three and 3¼hours running length.

Master First generation recording.

Mega (M) 1,000,000.

Micro (μ) 1/1,000,000.

Milli (m) 1/1,000.

Mode Operating position – play, rewind, record, etc.

Monitor Video display screen with no front-end tuning section.

NTSC National Television Standards Committee. Colour TV system used in USA and Japan.

Off-air recording Recording of broadcast programme.

Oracle IBA tradename for its television-linked teletext system.

PAL Phase Alternate Line. Colour TV system used in Britain.

Pan Swivelling of camera about a fixed axis.

Portapack Battery powered VTR and camera combination.

Prestel GPO trade name for its telephone-linked viewdata system.

Quadruplex 2 in video tape format developed by Ampex (USA).

Raw video Colloquial jargon for non RF-modulated picture signal.

Receiver Another name for conventional TV set. Unlike a *monitor*, it requires an RF-modulated sound and picture input.

RETRA Radio Electrical and Television Retailers Association.

RF Radio Frequency. An RF signal comprises radio frequency carriers modulated by sound and picture information. These carriers are removed at the input of a TV receiver, leaving separate video and sound components. Sole function of RF carriers is to make broadcasting of video and sound components possible. Each introduction or removal (encoding or decoding) of carriers degrades signal quality. Hence it is preferable to work with pure video and sound signal components in a closed system, for instance when copying.

Schmidt optics Three-tube system of video projection.

SECAM Sequential colour with memory. Colour TV system used in France.

Still frame Continuous reproduction of a stationary helical-scan video tape or the corresponding portion of a video disc.

SVR Obsolete ½ in video cassette format developed by Grundig (West Germany).

TeD Mechanically reproduced disc developed by Decca (Britain) and Telefunken (West Germany).

Telecine Device for replaying cine film over the television system.

Teletext Transmission of alphanumerics by radio, as in Ceefax and Oracle.

Time Code Binary code recorded on video or audio tape recorders which uniquely indentifies frames. Used professionally for synchronising recorders and editing.

Timer In home video, device to postpone recording from specified TV station until pre-selected time and day.

Timeshift Use of VTR to delay screening of TV programme output.

Tip projection Amount by which video head projects from head drum.

U-matic ¾ in video cassette format developed by Sony (Japan).

VCR, VCR-LP Video cassette ½ in format developed by Philips (Holland).

VDU Visual Display Unit. Usually describes plumbed-in CRT.

VHS ½ in video cassette format developed by JVC (Japan).

Vidicon TV camera tube employing photo-resistive image detector.

Viewdata Transmission of alphanumerics by wire, as in Prestel.

Viewfinder Visual guide to image in view, mounted in or adjacent to a TV camera.

VTR Video Tape Recorder.

Video 2000 Double sided video cassette format developed by Philips (Holland).

Wow Variation in speed of a recording medium, occurring between one and 15 times per second. See *Drift* and *Flutter*.

Zoom Movable element lens system giving adjustable magnification of image.

Supplier index

Akai (UK) Ltd,
12 Silver Jubilee Way,
Haslemere Heathrow Estate,
Hounslow, Middlesex, TW4 6NF.

Grundig (UK) Ltd,
Newlands Park,
London SE26 5NQ.

Hitachi Sales (UK) Ltd,
Hitachi House,
Station Road,
Hayes, Middlesex UB3 4DR.

ITT Consumer Products (UK) Ltd,
Chester Hall Lane,
Basildon, Essex.

JVC (UK) Ltd,
Eldonwall Trading Estate,
Staples Corner, London W2.

Mitsubishi Electric (UK) Ltd,
Otterspool Way,
Watford WD2 8LD.

Nordmende (UK) Ltd,
Aylesbury, Buckinghamshire
HP20 2RT.

Panasonic (UK) Ltd,
308–318 Bath Road,
Slough, SL3 6JB.

Philips Electrical Ltd,
19 Commerce Way,
Purley Way,
Croydon CR9 4JA.

Pye Ltd,
137 Ditton Walk,
Cambridge CB5 8QD.

Rank Radio International,
PO Box 196,
London W4 1PW.
(includes Bush, Rank, Arena)

Sharp Electronics (UK) Ltd,
Sharp House,
107 Hulme Hall Lane,
Manchester M10 8HL.

Sanyo (UK) Ltd,
8 Greycaine Road,
Watford WD2 4UQ.

Sony (UK) Ltd,
Pyrene House,
Sunbury Cross,
Sunbury-on-Thames,
Middlesex.